CONTENTS

48 AI FINANCE SECRETS

UNLEASHED

MASTERING THE PATH TO FINANCIAL
REVOLUTION

INTRODUCTION TO AI IN FINANCE

Overview of AI in the Financial Sector
In the financial industry, artificial intelligence (AI)

has become a potent instrument that is changing the way financial institutions function and the financial landscape as a whole. This chapter will give a general overview of artificial intelligence (AI) in the financial industry, examining its advantages, difficulties, and different approaches. We will also explore the ethical issues that come up when AI-driven finance is implemented.

The financial industry is typified by large data sets, intricate computations, and a pressing requirement for prompt decision-making. Artificial intelligence (AI) has become a crucial asset in this market due to its capacity to analyze enormous datasets, recognize trends, and make predictions. Financial institutions can improve their ability to make decisions, automate procedures, and obtain insightful knowledge by utilizing AI approaches.

AI has many advantages in the financial sector. The capability to produce market insights is one of the main benefits. Financial experts can spot trade signals, evaluate investor mood, and identify market trends with the help of predictive analytics, sentiment analysis, and pattern recognition techniques. These revelations can help with risk management, investing strategy, and decision-making in general.

Artificial Intelligence has also significantly enhanced automated investment tactics. Algorithmic trading, high-frequency trading, and robo-advisors are a few strategies that have become more well-known recently. Investors can now improve their portfolios, execute trades quickly, and better manage risk thanks to these AI-driven strategies.

Artificial intelligence has also changed personalized financial planning. AI-powered solutions enable people to manage spending, make smart budgets, set financial objectives, and prepare for retirement. These individualized programs offer specific recommendations and guidance based on each person's unique situation, risk tolerance, and financial goals.

Another area where AI has made a big impact is efficient data navigation. Financial institutions work with enormous volumes of data, and artificial intelligence (AI) tools like data mining, natural language processing, data visualization, and data collection and preprocessing help them draw valuable conclusions from this data. These methods aid in comprehending consumer behavior, market trends, and regulatory compliance.

Additionally, AI has made it possible to obtain financial insights that were previously unattainable. Artificial intelligence (AI) algorithms have simplified the loan approval and credit scoring processes, allowing financial firms to make more precise and effective decisions. Additionally improved are methods for preventing and detecting fraud, which enable organizations to properly identify and manage risks. AI has also been shown to be extremely important in regulatory compliance, making sure that financial firms follow the law and ethical guidelines.

AI has many advantages, but there are drawbacks and moral dilemmas as well. A difficulty is the requirement for high-quality data. Large datasets are necessary for AI systems to produce precise forecasts and judgments. Financial institutions must thus make sure that the data they employ is accurate, current, and representative of the intended audience.

The interpretability of AI models is another problem. AI algorithms frequently operate as "black boxes," making it challenging to decipher the logic underlying their judgments. Concerns concerning prejudice, justice, and responsibility are brought up by this lack of interpretability. To maintain openness and foster client trust, financial institutions must solve these problems.

AI-driven finance also places a high priority on ethical issues. Concerns of employment displacement, security, and privacy are brought up by the application of AI algorithms. In order to guarantee that AI is applied ethically and in the best interests of their clients, financial institutions must resolve these moral conundrums.

We will go into great detail about the various

AI methods applied in finance, as well as their uses and real-world examples, in the upcoming chapters. Along with talking about potential future developments and prospects in AI finance, we will also offer doable tactics for integrating AI in financial institutions. Readers will have a thorough understanding of artificial intelligence (AI) in finance by the end of the book, and they will be prepared to handle the AI-driven financial transformation with knowledge and insights.

AI's advantages and difficulties in finance

In the financial industry, artificial intelligence (AI) has become a potent instrument that is changing both the way individuals manage their finances and how financial institutions function. Although integrating AI into finance has several advantages, there are a number of issues that must be resolved. This section will examine the advantages and difficulties of artificial intelligence (AI) in finance, offering a thorough grasp of the sector's effects.

- AI's Advantages for Finance
  1. Increased precision and effectiveness
  The capacity of AI to improve accuracy and efficiency across a range of financial procedures is one of the main

advantages for the banking industry. By automating monotonous processes like data entry and analysis, AI-powered algorithms free up financial professionals' time to concentrate on more intricate and strategic work. Artificial intelligence enhances financial decision-making speed and accuracy by decreasing human errors and optimizing processes.

- 2. Enhanced client relationship
Financial organizations can now provide their clients with individualized and customized services thanks to AI technologies. AI algorithms can recognize unique tastes, behaviors, and financial objectives through the analysis of enormous volumes of data. This capability enables the provision of personalized recommendations and solutions. This customized strategy improves the client experience as a whole, which raises client happiness and loyalty.

- 3. Improved Risk Administration
In the financial industry, artificial intelligence is vital to risk management. Artificial intelligence systems have the ability to anticipate

and reduce hazards by examining past data and spotting trends. This covers spotting irregularities in financial transactions, credit ratings, and fraud detection. Financial organizations can lessen the chance of monetary losses and reputational harm by using AI to proactively manage risks.

- 4. Better Decision-Making: Artificial intelligence provides finance professionals with strong decision-making skills. Artificial intelligence (AI) systems are able to make insightful predictions by sifting through enormous volumes of data and looking for patterns. Financial institutions can use this information to make well-informed decisions on risk management, investments, and portfolio management. Making decisions with AI drives more precise and profitable results.

- 5. Saving Money
There can be large cost savings in the banking industry by implementing AI technologies. Financial institutions can save on operating costs and require fewer human resources by automating manual processes and optimizing operations. AI can also find

inefficiencies and optimize resource distribution, which lowers prices even further. Financial services will become more reasonably priced as a result of these cost savings being transferred to clients

- **AI's Difficulties in Finance**
  1. Availability and Quality of Data
  The availability and quality of data are two of the main obstacles facing AI in banking. Large amounts of high-quality data are necessary for AI systems to produce precise insights and forecasts. Financial data, however, can be error-prone, complex, and unstructured. Achieving data availability and quality is essential to the application of AI in banking.

- 2. Moral Aspects
  There are ethical questions raised by the application of AI in finance that require discussion. Unfair results may result from AI systems that unintentionally reinforce biases found in the data they are trained on. Concerns regarding discrimination and privacy are also raised by the application of AI in processes like loan approval and credit scoring. To guarantee the ethical and

just application of AI technologies, financial institutions must create moral frameworks and policies.

- 3. Adherence to Regulations
The use of AI in banking brings with it new difficulties for regulatory compliance. Financial organizations are required to make sure AI algorithms abide by current laws and guidelines. This covers adherence to data protection regulations, the explainability of AI models, and openness in decision-making. Respecting legal mandates is essential to preserving confidence in AI-powered financial systems.

- 4. Dangers to Cybersecurity
Cybersecurity risks rise in tandem with AI's increasing use in banking. Attacks like adversarial and data breach assaults can happen to AI systems. To safeguard sensitive financial data and guarantee the accuracy and dependability of AI systems, financial institutions need to make significant investments in cybersecurity measures.

- 5. Adaptation of the Workforce
The workforce's roles and skill set must change in order for AI to be fully

integrated into finance. While AI can automate some processes, it also opens up new possibilities and raises the need for specialized knowledge. Financial professionals must learn about artificial intelligence (AI) in order to keep up with the rapidly evolving field. Programs for reskilling and upskilling are necessary to guarantee a seamless transition and optimize the advantages of AI in banking.

In conclusion, there are several advantages to integrating AI into finance, such as increased productivity, better risk management, and an improved customer experience. Nevertheless, it poses obstacles to data quality, ethical issues, regulatory adherence, cybersecurity threats, and worker flexibility. Financial institutions may fully utilize AI to spur innovation and industry transformation by tackling these obstacles and capitalizing on its advantages.

- AI Methods Applied to Finance

The financial industry has undergone a revolution thanks to artificial intelligence (AI), which has introduced a wide range of tools that have changed how financial institutions function. This chapter will examine some of the most important artificial intelligence (AI) techniques utilized in the banking sector and how they are enhancing industry insights and tactics.

Artificial Intelligence

A kind of artificial intelligence called machine learning (ML) gives computers the ability to learn and make judgments without explicit programming. Machine learning algorithms are employed in the financial industry to examine vast amounts of data and detect trends or patterns that have several applications. ML algorithms, for instance, can be used to evaluate credit risk, detect trade signals, and forecast market movements.

Supervised learning is a well-liked machine learning technique in the finance industry, where algorithms are trained on labeled data to provide predictions or classifications. For example, machine learning algorithms can be trained on past data to estimate the probability of a borrower defaulting on a loan in the context of a credit rating. Unsupervised learning is another machine learning method used in finance, in which algorithms examine unlabeled data to find trends or clusters. Finding irregularities in financial transactions can be helpful in the discovery of fraud.

In-depth Education

A branch of machine learning called deep learning (DL) aims to teach artificial neural networks to learn and behave like human brains. When it comes to processing and analyzing vast volumes of unstructured data, including text, audio, or photos, DL algorithms are especially useful. Deep learning techniques have been used in finance for a number of purposes, such as sentiment analysis, fraud detection, and natural language processing.

Sentiment analysis is the process of examining textual data—such as posts on social media or news articles—to ascertain the sentiment or viewpoint that is being communicated. Investors can assess market sentiment and make wise judgments by teaching DL algorithms to comprehend the sentiment and context of financial news stories. In order to help algorithms recognize patterns or irregularities in financial transactions that can point to fraudulent activity, DL techniques have also been applied to fraud detection.

Understanding Natural Language
A subfield of artificial intelligence called natural language processing, or NLP, is concerned with how computers and human language interact. NLP approaches are applied in the banking industry to evaluate and comprehend textual data, including news articles, financial reports, and consumer feedback. NLP algorithms allow computers to comprehend and respond to human language, extract pertinent information, and identify important entities or concepts.

Automated news analysis is one way that NLP

is used in the financial sector. NLP algorithms may extract important information from financial news stories, such as economic data or corporate results, and instantly deliver investor insights. Additionally, NLP approaches can be applied in customer service, wherein chatbots or virtual assistants can comprehend and reply to client inquiries, as well as offer tailored financial guidance.

Learning via Reinforcement

An ML technique called reinforcement learning (RL) teaches an agent to make decisions by letting it interact with its surroundings and giving it feedback in the form of incentives or penalties. In dynamic and uncertain contexts like financial markets, where the best course of action may alter over time, reinforcement learning algorithms (RL) are very helpful. Algorithmic trading and portfolio optimization are two financial objectives for which reinforcement learning techniques have been used.

RL algorithms are able to learn how to distribute investments across various assets in portfolio optimization, maximizing returns while controlling risk. RL algorithms are able to optimize investment strategies and adjust to changing market conditions by continuously learning from market data and modifying the portfolio allocation. In algorithmic trading, where algorithms are trained to make buy or sell decisions based on market data and past performance, reinforcement learning techniques have also been applied.

Automation of Robotic Processes

Software robots, sometimes known as "bots," are used in robotic process automation (RPA) technologies to automate repetitive and rule-based processes. RPA techniques are utilized in finance to automate back-office tasks like data input, reconciliation, and report preparation. Financial organizations can increase productivity, lower errors, and free up human resources for higher-value work by automating certain processes.

Financial report generation, data validation, and data extraction from financial statements are among the jobs that RPA bots can be trained to accomplish. These bots are able to operate around the clock, making sure that tasks are finished precisely and on schedule. To further improve automation capabilities in finance, RPA techniques can also be linked with other AI approaches, including ML or NLP.

Algorithmic Genetics

Natural selection serves as the inspiration for genetic algorithms (GA), which are methods of optimization. GA algorithms are especially helpful in resolving intricate optimization issues involving numerous constraints and variables. GA approaches have been used in finance for a number of purposes, such as risk management, trading strategy optimization, and portfolio optimization.

GA algorithms can be used in portfolio optimization to find the best asset combination to maximize returns and minimize risk. Through the consideration of multiple parameters, including correlation, historical performance, and risk tolerance, a genetic algorithm (GA) can produce portfolios that are both diversified and efficient. By identifying the ideal set of criteria or regulations to maximize profit, GA techniques can also be used to optimize trading strategies.

These are but a handful of the AI methods employed in the financial industry. The topic of artificial intelligence (AI) in finance is developing quickly, and new methods are always being created and used to tackle challenging financial issues. Financial institutions may automate procedures, obtain insightful knowledge, and make better judgments in the data-driven, fast-paced world of finance by utilizing these AI strategies.

Ethical Aspects of AI-Powered Finance
It is critical to address the ethical issues raised by the application of artificial intelligence (AI) in banking as the financial sector continues to adopt these technologies. Although AI has the ability to completely transform the industry and offer a host of advantages, there are hazards and difficulties that must be properly addressed. In this section, we will look at some of the most important ethical issues in AI-driven finance and talk about solutions.

- Explainability and Transparency
The lack of explainability and transparency in AI algorithms is one of the main ethical issues in AI-driven finance. A lot of artificial intelligence models, including deep learning neural networks, are referred to as "black boxes" since their judgments are based on intricate relationships and patterns that are challenging to understand. Concerns about accountability and the possibility of unfair or biased results are raised by this lack of transparency.

Financial institutions should work to create AI models that are transparent and comprehensible in order to allay this worry. This can be accomplished by using strategies like model interpretability, which enables stakeholders to comprehend the AI model's decision-making process. Financial institutions may boost trust and guarantee impartiality and fairness by offering explanations and justifications for AI-driven judgments.

- Security and Privacy of Data
The preservation of data security and privacy is a crucial ethical factor in AI-driven finance. For AI systems to produce precise forecasts and judgments, enormous volumes of data are required. The security and privacy of sensitive financial data are questioned in light of the increasing reliance on data.

Financial institutions need to put strong data protection procedures in place and give priority to data security and privacy. This entails putting robust encryption and access control systems in place as well as making sure that pertinent data protection laws, such as the General Data Protection Regulation (GDPR), are followed. Financial firms should also have customers' express consent for data collection and processing and be open and honest about how their data is utilized.

- Fairness and Bias

The objectivity of AI algorithms is dependent on the quality of the training data. Unfair results may result from AI models that reinforce and magnify biases present in the training data. Biased AI algorithms in the financial sector may lead to unfair lending practices, unequal access to financial services, and other financial injustices.

Financial institutions should carefully choose and preprocess their training data to remove any biases in order to assure fairness and mitigate bias. Additionally, they must routinely check for bias in their AI models through audits and monitoring and, when needed, take remedial action. Incorporating diverse teams into the creation and evaluation of AI algorithms can also aid in locating and resolving such biases.

- Responsibility and Accountability
AI-driven finance calls into question responsibility and accountability. When an AI algorithm makes a bad choice or does damage, who is accountable? Which party should bear more of the burden: the AI, the financial institutions, or the developers?

Financial institutions should set up distinct roles and responsibilities for AI-driven systems in order to allay these worries. Determining the functions and duties of developers, data scientists, and decision-makers falls under this category. Financial institutions should also have systems in place to keep an eye on, audit, and take appropriate corrective action when needed about the performance of AI algorithms.

- Human Supervision and Management
Even though many financial decisions and processes can be automated by AI algorithms, human monitoring and control must still be maintained. Humans possess critical thinking, empathy, and ethical reasoning skills that are essential in the financial sector.

Financial organizations need to make sure AI solutions are made to support human judgment rather than completely replace it. Human-in-the-loop techniques, in which people examine and approve the judgments rendered by AI algorithms, can help achieve this. Financial institutions can guarantee that AI-driven finance is morally righteous and consistent with human ideals by retaining human monitoring and management.

- Constant observation and adjustment
AI-driven finance involves dynamic ethical considerations that change over time. Financial institutions need to be on the lookout for new hazards and constantly review and modify their ethical frameworks and procedures as AI technologies progress.

Financial organizations ought to set up strong governance structures that involve routinely observing and assessing AI systems. This involves interacting with stakeholders, carrying out ethical effect analyses, and keeping abreast of the most recent advancements in AI ethics. Financial institutions may guarantee that AI-driven finance stays morally sound and consistent with societal norms by closely observing and modifying their operations on a regular basis.

In summary, even though artificial intelligence (AI) has the potential to completely transform the financial sector, there are important ethical issues that need to be addressed. To guarantee that AI-driven finance is morally righteous and advantageous for all parties involved, financial institutions need to concentrate on a number of important areas, including transparency and explainability, data privacy and security, bias and fairness, accountability and responsibility, human oversight and control, and ongoing monitoring and adaptation. Financial organizations may foster a more ethical and sustainable financial ecosystem, increase consumer happiness, and foster trust by proactively addressing these ethical factors.

AI FOR MARKET INSIGHTS

- Market Trend Predictive Analytics
Financial institutions now monitor and interpret

market movements in a completely new way, thanks to the potent AI approach known as predictive analytics. Finance professionals can anticipate future market moves and make well-informed judgments by using predictive analytics, which makes use of historical data, statistical algorithms, and machine learning models.

Gaining Knowledge about Predictive Analytics
Utilizing past data to find patterns, connections, and trends that can be utilized to forecast future events is known as predictive analytics. This method enables traders and analysts to predict market trends, spot possible investment opportunities, and reduce risks in the financial domain.

Predictive analytics usually requires a number of steps. First, past data is gathered from multiple sources, including financial markets, economic indicators, and the financial statements of businesses. After that, this data is cleansed and preprocessed to guarantee its accuracy. The data is then subjected to statistical and machine learning algorithms in order to find patterns and linkages. These models are used to forecast new, unseen data after being trained on historical data.

Financial Predictive Analytics Methods
In the financial industry, a number of predictive analytics methods are frequently employed. Among these methods are:

Analysis of the Time Series

A statistical method for analyzing and projecting data points gathered over time is time series analysis. Time series analysis is widely used in finance to forecast exchange rates, stock prices, and other financial indicators. Traders and analysts can forecast future market trends by examining past price movements and spotting trends.

Analysis of Regression

A statistical method for simulating the relationship between a dependent variable and one or more independent variables is regression analysis. Regression analysis is a common tool in finance used to forecast an asset's value based on a variety of variables, including interest rates, economic indicators, and the financials of the organization. Analysts can forecast future market trends by examining past data and determining the correlation between various variables.

Networks of neural

One kind of machine learning model that draws inspiration from the composition and operations of the human brain is the neural network. Neural networks are widely used in finance to forecast credit risk, stock prices, and other financial metrics. A neural network can be trained on past data to identify intricate patterns and relationships that enable the model to forecast new, unobserved data with accuracy.

Group Approaches

Several predictive models are used in ensemble methods to increase forecast resilience and accuracy. Ensemble methods are widely used in finance to forecast market trends and guide investment decisions. Through the integration of various models' projections, analysts can mitigate the danger of erroneous forecasts and enhance the probability of pinpointing lucrative investment prospects.

Finance's Gains from Predictive Analytics

The financial industry benefits greatly from predictive analytics in a number of ways. Among them are:

Better Ability to Make Decisions

Financial organizations may make better-informed, data-driven decisions by utilizing predictive analytics. Analysts can forecast future market movements by examining historical data, seeing patterns and trends, and mitigating risks. This allows them to make smarter investment judgments.

Improved Risk Administration

Financial organizations can more efficiently detect and manage risks with the aid of predictive analytics. Analysts can spot possible hazards and take proactive steps to reduce them by looking for patterns and trends in past data. This can enhance general risk management techniques and help avoid monetary losses.

Enhanced Effectiveness
Numerous financial procedures can be automated and streamlined with predictive analytics, increasing productivity and lowering costs. Financial organizations can free up critical time and resources by automating processes like data collection, preparation, and analysis. This allows them to concentrate on more strategic endeavors.

An edge over competitors
Financial institutions can obtain a competitive edge in the market by utilizing predictive analytics. Institutions can beat their rivals and draw in more customers by improving their forecasting skills and spotting lucrative investment opportunities.

Finance's Predictive Analytics Challenges
Even if predictive analytics has many advantages, there are certain issues that must be resolved. Among these difficulties are:

Data accessibility and quality
Predictive analytics methods rely heavily on the availability and quality of data. The accuracy, dependability, and timeliness of the data used by financial institutions must be guaranteed. Furthermore, it can be difficult to obtain pertinent data because financial information is frequently dispersed across several sources and can be labor-

intensive to gather and prepare.

Interpretability and Complexity of the Model
Neural networks are one type of predictive analytics model that can be quite sophisticated and challenging to understand. Because of this, financial institutions may find it difficult to comprehend and justify the assumptions underlying the models' forecasts. Maintaining the interpretability of the models is crucial to fostering faith and assurance in the forecasts they generate.

Generalization and Overfitting
When a predictive model works well on training data but is unable to generalize to new, untested data, this is known as overfitting. This may result in erroneous forecasts and untrustworthy outcomes. For their prediction models to be reliable and able to generalize to new data, financial institutions must thoroughly assess and validate them.

Moral Aspects to Take into Account
Ethics are raised by predictive analytics in finance, especially when it comes to loan approval and credit scoring. Predictive models must be made sure to be impartial, fair, and free from discrimination against any particular people or groups. Furthermore, careful handling and adherence to applicable privacy requirements are required when using sensitive financial information, including personal information.

To sum up, the application of predictive analytics is a potent AI method that has revolutionized the way financial organizations assess and understand market patterns. Finance workers may reduce risks, make well-informed decisions, and predict future market moves by using predictive analytics, which makes use of historical data as well as sophisticated statistical and machine learning models. However, to guarantee the efficacy and dependability of predictive analytics in finance, it is crucial to address issues including data quality, model complexity, overfitting, and ethical considerations.

- Financial Market Sentiment Analysis

Opinion mining, or sentiment analysis, is a potent AI approach that is transforming the understanding and analysis of financial markets. Monetary research offers important insights into investor behavior and market mood by examining and evaluating the sentiment expressed in a variety of data sources, including news stories, social media posts, and financial reports. This section will examine the applications of sentiment analysis in the financial markets and the advantages it provides to financial institutions and investors.

Comprehending Sentiment Analysis

Sentiment analysis is the practice of extracting and analyzing subjective information from textual data using natural language processing (NLP) tools. It seeks to ascertain the sentiment—whether good, negative, or neutral—expressed in a given text. Sentiment analysis in the context of financial markets is concerned with obtaining sentiment toward particular financial instruments, businesses, or market patterns.

Sources of Attitude Information

Financial market sentiment analysis collects sentiment data from a variety of data sources. Among these sources are:

News Articles: Reputable sources of financial news articles offer insightful analyses of market sentiment. Investors can gain a better grasp of how news events and market developments are influencing investor sentiment by examining the sentiment represented in these articles.

Social Media: Sites like Facebook and Twitter have developed into rich sources of sentimental information. Sentiment analysis is a real-time tool for gaining insights into investor sentiment and market trends by examining the sentiment expressed in financial market-related social media posts.

Financial Reports: Financial reports, including analyst and earnings reports, can also be subjected to sentiment analysis. Investors can learn about the opinions of financial analysts and market specialists by examining the sentiments represented in these publications.

Online Forums and Discussion Boards: Financial markets-focused online forums and discussion boards offer a plethora of sentiment information. Sentiment analysis can shed light on the attitudes of retail traders and investors by examining the opinions posted in these forums.

Sentiment Analysis's Advantages for the Financial Markets
When it comes to comprehending and evaluating financial markets, sentiment analysis provides investors and financial organizations with a number of advantages. Among the main advantages are:

Market Sentiment Analysis: Sentiment analysis can shed light on market sentiment by examining sentiment data from a variety of sources. Investors can use this data to determine how the public feels generally about particular financial products, businesses, or market movements.

Early Market Trend Identification: Investors can benefit from sentiment analysis by being able to recognize new market trends early on. Investors can make well-informed investing decisions by detecting changes in sentiment towards particular sectors or companies through the analysis of sentiment data.

Sentiment analysis is another tool that can be utilized in risk management. Financial organizations can detect such hazards and take appropriate action to mitigate them by keeping an eye on sentiment data.

Trading Strategies: Trading strategies based on market sentiment can be created using sentiment analysis. Investors can potentially enhance their trading performance and make better selections by integrating sentiment data into trading models.

Sentiment analysis's limitations and challenges Although sentiment research provides insightful information about the financial markets, it is not without its own set of difficulties and restrictions. Among the principal difficulties are:

Data Quality: The degree of sentiment data varies greatly throughout sources. Ensuring the accuracy and dependability of sentiment data utilized for analysis is crucial.

Sentiment analysis algorithms frequently encounter difficulties in comprehending the context in which sentiment is expressed. Results from sentiment analysis may become erroneous as a result.

Social Media Data Noise: A substantial amount of unnecessary information can be found in social media data, which can be noisy. It can be difficult to remove noise and retrieve pertinent sentiment data.

Linguistic and Cultural Differences: In order to effectively assess sentiment in various markets and areas, sentiment analysis algorithms must take linguistic and cultural differences into consideration.

Upcoming Developments in Sentiment Analysis
Sentiment analysis in financial markets is anticipated to grow increasingly complex and precise as AI develops. Future directions in sentiment analysis could include the following:

Sentiment analysis algorithms are developing to understand the underlying emotions portrayed in text as well as to detect sentiment. A deeper understanding of investor behavior and market sentiment may result from this.

Multimodal Sentiment Analysis: As multimedia data, including photos and videos, becomes more widely available, sentiment analysis is expanding to include sentiment expressed in these formats. This may offer a more thorough comprehension of market moods.

Real-time sentiment analysis: In the financial markets, real-time sentiment analysis is becoming more and more significant. Investors can make more educated and fast judgments by using real-time sentiment data analysis.

Integration with Other AI Techniques: To offer more thorough market insights, sentiment analysis is being combined with other AI techniques like pattern recognition and predictive analytics.

In summary, sentiment analysis is a potent AI method that is revolutionizing the comprehension and analysis of financial markets. Sentiment analysis offers important insights into market sentiment, early trend recognition, and risk management by examining sentiment data from multiple sources. Although sentiment analysis has its own set of drawbacks and difficulties, developments in AI are anticipated to solve these issues and improve sentiment analysis's precision and efficacy in the financial markets.

- Identifying Patterns in Trading Signals
One of the most important aspects of trading in financial markets is recognizing patterns. To

find possible trading opportunities, traders and investors are always looking for patterns in volume, price fluctuations, and other market indicators. But the human brain is not designed to comprehend large amounts of data or identify intricate patterns. Artificial intelligence (AI) can help in this situation by providing strong instruments for trading signal pattern detection.

Recognizing Financial Market Trends

Numerous factors, such as economic indicators, geopolitical developments, investor emotion, and market psychology, influence the financial markets. The price movements of different financial assets, including stocks, bonds, currencies, and commodities, exhibit patterns due to these causes. Finding and comprehending these trends might offer insightful information that will help you make wise trading selections.

Financial markets can exhibit a variety of patterns, such as trend, reversal, and continuation patterns. The market's trend tells us whether it is heading higher (bullish) or lower (bearish). While continuation patterns show that the current trend is likely to continue, reversal patterns hint at a possible change in the market's direction.

Conventional Methods for Pattern Identification

Traders used manual analysis and technical indicators to find patterns in trading signals prior to the development of artificial intelligence. Technical indicators were employed to identify possible trading opportunities. These indicators included oscillators, moving averages, and chart patterns. However, the accuracy and efficiency of these conventional methods were limited.

The process of manually analyzing trading signals takes a lot of time and is subject to prejudice. Traders could make less-than-ideal trading judgments if they overlook or misread significant patterns. In addition, conventional technical indicators frequently lag behind the market, which makes it challenging to seize trade opportunities in real time.

Pattern Recognition Driven by AI
AI has transformed trading signal pattern recognition by utilizing cutting-edge algorithms and machine learning strategies. Large volumes of past market data can be analyzed by machine learning algorithms, which can then use the patterns they find to forecast future market movements.

Neural networks are a common method for pattern identification in trading signals. Inspired by the structure and functions of the human brain, neural networks are computer models made up of interconnected nodes, or neurons, that process and transmit data. Neural networks can be trained on past market data to identify intricate patterns and produce trading signals.

Genetic algorithms are another AI method for

trading signal pattern recognition. To maximize trading tactics, genetic algorithms simulate the process of natural selection. They create a population of trading strategies with various parameters and use past data to assess how well they perform. The trading strategies that perform the best are chosen and blended to produce new generations of methods that steadily get better over time.

Advantages of Pattern Recognition Driven by AI
Financial market traders and investors can profit from AI-powered pattern detection in a number of ways. First off, real-time processing of enormous volumes of data by AI algorithms makes it possible for traders to swiftly spot trends and produce trading recommendations. In quick-moving markets, this speed and effectiveness provide traders with a competitive advantage.

Second, complicated patterns that humans might find difficult to identify can be analyzed by AI algorithms. Their ability to spot minute dependencies and correlations in market data results in trading signals that are more precise. Traders can find fresh trading opportunities and enhance their trading tactics by using this capacity to uncover hidden patterns.

Moreover, pattern identification enabled by AI can lessen human prejudice in trading choices. Irrational trading decisions might result from emotional and cognitive biases impairing judgment. Contrarily, AI algorithms eliminate emotional biases and increase the consistency of trading methods by basing their conclusions on an objective study of facts.

Obstacles and Things to Think About

Although pattern recognition enabled by AI has many benefits, there are drawbacks and things to keep in mind. First and foremost, the caliber and consistency of the data utilized to train AI systems are essential. Reliable and precise data are necessary for algorithms to be trained to identify significant trends. Thus, in the process of using AI to power pattern recognition, quality assurance and data pretreatment are essential phases.

Second, a common issue with AI-powered pattern recognition is overfitting. When an algorithm becomes very specialized in identifying patterns in the training data but is unable to generalize successfully to new, unseen data, this is known as overfitting. In order to prevent overfitting and to make sure that their AI algorithms are resilient and able to adjust to shifting market conditions, traders and investors must exercise caution.

Last but not least, applying AI-powered pattern recognition to trading signals requires careful consideration of ethical issues. To enable traders to comprehend the logic underlying the trading signals that are generated, AI systems must be transparent and comprehensible. Furthermore, appropriate risk management techniques must be used to reduce any possible dangers connected to trading decisions made by AI.

In summary, trading in financial markets is being revolutionized by AI-powered pattern identification. Traders and investors are able to recognize intricate patterns in trading signals and make well-informed trading decisions by utilizing sophisticated algorithms and machine learning approaches. However, to guarantee the efficacy and dependability of AI-powered pattern recognition in finance, it is crucial to address issues like data quality, overfitting, and moral considerations.

- Market forecasting driven by AI
An essential component of finance that aids in the decision-making of financial institutions and investors is market forecasting. Market

forecasting has historically been based on expert analysis, statistical models, and historical data. But market forecasting has changed dramatically since artificial intelligence (AI) emerged, offering more precise and timely insights.

Artificial intelligence (AI)-powered market forecasting uses sophisticated algorithms and machine learning techniques to examine enormous volumes of data and spot patterns and trends that human analysts would miss. AI models may produce predictions and projections with a higher degree of accuracy by processing and analyzing data from a variety of sources, including financial statements, news articles, social media, and economic indicators.

Artificial Intelligence Models for Market Prediction

In AI-powered market forecasting, machine learning models are essential. These models use historical data to forecast future market patterns by learning from it. In market forecasting, a number of well-liked machine learning algorithms are employed, such as:

Models of Regression

In market forecasting, regression models are frequently used to project a financial asset's future value using previous data. In order to produce forecasts, these models examine the link between the independent variables—such as corporate financials and economic indicators

—and the dependent variable, such as stock price. Regression techniques that are frequently employed in market forecasting include support vector, polynomial, and linear regression.

Analysis of Time Series

A statistical method for analyzing and projecting data points gathered over time is time series analysis. Time series analysis methods are useful in market forecasting because they can capture the cyclical variations and seasonal patterns that are inherent in financial data. Popular time series analysis methods used in market forecasting include exponential smoothing (ES) and autoregressive integrated moving averages (ARIMA).

Inverse Structures

A class of machine learning models called neural networks is modeled after the composition and operations of the human brain. These models have the ability to recognize intricate relationships and patterns in the data. Neural networks—such as feedforward and recurrent neural networks (RNNs)—are capable of accurately predicting nonlinear relationships and making accurate predictions in the field of market forecasting. In tasks involving market forecasting, deep learning methods like long short-term memory (LSTM) networks and convolutional neural networks (CNNs) have also demonstrated promise.

Data Sources for Market Forecasting Driven by AI

AI models need access to a variety of data sources in order to produce precise market forecasts. These resources offer insightful data on economic indicators, investor mood, corporate financials, and market circumstances. Typical data sources for AI-powered market forecasting include the following:

Monetary Information

Economic indicators, past stock prices, and corporate financial statements are examples of financial data that can be used to get important insights into market conditions and trends. This data can be analyzed by AI models to find connections and patterns that can be utilized to provide forecasts.

Social Media and News

Financial markets can be impacted by a multitude of pieces of information found in news stories and on social media sites. In order to determine investor mood, spot new trends, and evaluate how news events affect market movements, AI algorithms can examine news articles and social media posts.

Supplementary Information

Non-traditional data sources that offer distinctive insights into market patterns are referred to as alternative data. This comprises sensor data, credit card transaction data, online scraping, and satellite imagery data. Alternative data sources can be analyzed by AI models to find hidden trends and produce more precise market projections.

- Advantages and Drawbacks of AI-Powered Market Forecasting Compared to conventional techniques, AI-powered market forecasting has a number of advantages. Among the principal benefits are:

- Enhanced Precision
Large volumes of data can be processed and analyzed by AI models very quickly, which allows them to spot intricate patterns and trends that human analysts might miss. This results in more precise market projections and knowledgeable investing choices.

- Quick Snapshots
Real-time data from multiple sources can be analyzed by AI models, giving investors rapid insights into market conditions and trends. This makes it possible to make decisions more quickly and take advantage of new chances.

- Efficiency and Automation
Market forecasting driven by AI reduces the time and effort needed by human analysts by automating data analysis and prediction. Financial organizations can now examine more data and produce forecasts more quickly as a result.

AI-powered market forecasting has certain drawbacks, despite these advantages. Among them are:

- Restrictions on Data
The availability and quality of data are critical components of AI models. Predictions that are prejudiced or untrustworthy can result from incomplete or inaccurate data. To provide accurate market forecasting, data sources must be of high caliber and dependable.

- Interpretability of the Model
AI models can be complicated and challenging to understand, especially deep learning models. This lack of interpretability may reduce analysts' confidence in the model's predictions and make it difficult for them to comprehend the underlying variables driving the forecasts.

- Case Studies: Implementing AI-Powered Market Forecasting
AI-powered market forecasting has been shown to be effective in a number of real-world scenarios. For example, AI models are being used more and more by hedge funds and investment organizations to produce trade signals and make investment choices. To spot market patterns and provide effective trading techniques, these programs examine a ton of financial data as well as news items.

The application of sentiment analysis to market forecasting is another illustration. AI models are able to forecast market movements and assess investor mood by examining news articles and social media posts. Traders and investors hoping to profit from market moods may find this information useful.

In summary

By offering more precise and timely insights into market conditions and trends, AI-powered market forecasting has the potential to completely transform the financial industry. Artificial intelligence (AI) models can produce projections that assist financial institutions and investors in making well-informed decisions by utilizing sophisticated machine learning algorithms and evaluating large volumes of data. The drawbacks and difficulties of using AI to forecast markets, such as issues with data quality and model interpretability, must be taken into account. In the constantly changing financial landscape, investors and financial institutions can greatly benefit from the use of AI-powered market forecasts.

AUTOMATED INVESTMENT STRATEGIES

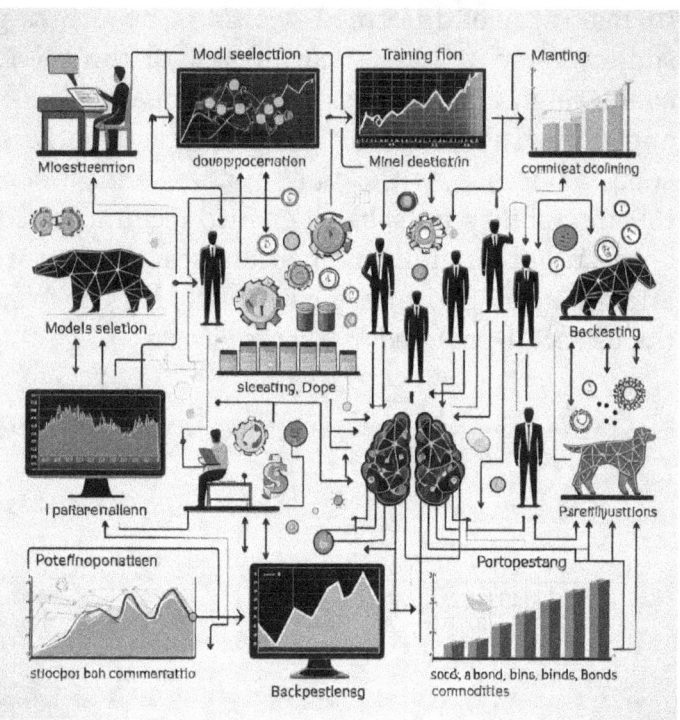

3.1 AI-powered investments and robot advisors

In the financial sector, robo-advisors have changed the game by transforming how people invest their money. Artificial intelligence (AI) algorithms are used by these automated investment platforms to manage investor portfolios and offer individualized investment advice. This section will examine the idea of robo-advisors and examine how artificial intelligence is raising the bar on investments.

3.1.1 Comprehending Automated Advisors

Online services known as "robo-advisors" automate financial operations through the use of AI algorithms. They provide people an easy and affordable option to invest their money. Usually, these platforms use an online questionnaire to collect data regarding an investor's investment choices, risk tolerance, and financial objectives. The robo-advisor algorithm uses this data to create a customized investment strategy based on the needs of the user.

Effective asset allocation and portfolio management are made possible by the application of AI in robo-advisors. To make wise investing selections, the computers examine a ton of financial data, market patterns, and past performance. Robo-advisors are able to provide investors with a degree of sophistication and precision that was previously exclusive to institutional investors or high-net-worth individuals by utilizing artificial intelligence.

3.1.2 Advantages of Virtual Advisors
Robo-advisors are a desirable choice for both inexperienced and seasoned investors due to their many advantages. Here are a few main benefits:

1. affordability and accessibility
Investing now has far lower entry barriers thanks to robo-advisors. They make it possible for people with little money or financial expertise to obtain expert investing advice and services. For a variety of investors, robo-advisors are an economical alternative due to their low costs and minimal investment requirements.

2. Individualization and Tailoring
Personalized investing plans are offered by AI-powered robo-advisors depending on a client's financial objectives, risk tolerance, and time horizon. To generate a customized investment strategy, the algorithms consider a number of variables, including age, income, and investing preferences. This degree of personalization guarantees that the investment plan corresponds with the investor's unique requirements and goals.

3. Risk management and diversification
Diversifying investing portfolios to reduce risk is a strength of robo-advisors. The algorithms distribute investments among various industries, regions, and asset kinds after analyzing a broad

range of asset classes. Robo-advisors can lessen the impact of market volatility and the risk associated with individual investments by distributing investments over a variety of assets.

4. Openness and Management

Investors have control and transparency over their money thanks to robo-advisors. Real-time access to transaction history, portfolio holdings, and investment performance is provided via the platforms. Investors are able to keep an eye on their portfolios and make modifications as needed. Furthermore, robo-advisors ensure that investors have a thorough understanding of their assets by offering reports that are simple to read and comprehend.

3.1.3 Restrictions and Difficulties

Although robo-advisors have many advantages, it's vital to understand their drawbacks and difficulties. Here are some things to think about:

1. Insufficient Human Engagement

Since robo-advisors are mainly technology-driven platforms, they don't offer the same level of personalization as traditional financial advisors. Working directly with a human advisor provides individualized assistance and emotional support, which may be preferred by certain investors. Whether or not to utilize a robo-advisor depends on a number of factors, including technological comfort and personal preferences.

2. The Risks of Algorithms and Market Volatility

Algorithms are used by robot advisers to make investing judgments. Even though these algorithms are made to examine past data and market trends, they might not always be able to forecast future changes in the market. The algorithms might not react appropriately during times of high market volatility or unforeseen events, which could result in worse than ideal investing outcomes.

3. Limited Opportunities for Investment

Exchange-traded funds (ETFs) and other pre-selected investment portfolios are commonly offered by robo-advisors. Although this offers diversification, investors who would rather invest in individual equities or particular asset classes may have fewer possibilities for making investments. The narrow selection of possibilities offered by robo-advisors may be limiting for investors with certain investing methods or preferences.

3.1.4 Robo-Advisors' Future

Robo-advisors appear to have a bright future thanks to ongoing developments in AI and machine learning. The following are some possible developments to be aware of:

1. Increased Customization

Robo-advisors will probably provide ever-higher levels of personalization as AI algorithms advance. To develop investing strategies that are consistent with a person's values and beliefs, the algorithms may take into account extra variables, such as social and environmental preferences.

2. Behavioral Finance Integrated
The study of psychological biases and emotions that affect investing decisions is known as behavioral finance. In order to better analyze investor behavior and adjust investing strategies, future robo-advisors might use behavioral finance concepts. This may assist investors in avoiding typical behavioral errors and making more logical investment choices.

3. Mixture Models
We may witness the rise of hybrid models that mix the advantages of robo-advisors with human experience in order to overcome the shortcomings of entirely technologically driven platforms. In addition to using AI algorithms for data analysis and portfolio management, these hybrid models would give users access to human advisors for individualized advice and support.

In summary, AI-powered robo-advisors have revolutionized the investing space by opening up access to expert portfolio management and investment advice to a larger market. Despite the fact that robo-advisors have many advantages, investors should weigh their objectives, risk tolerance, and personal preferences before using one. Robo-advisors are expected to develop further, providing even more customization and integration with human expertise as technology advances.

3.2 High-frequency trading and algorithmic trading

High-frequency trading (HFT) and algorithmic trading are two effective uses of artificial intelligence (AI) in the financial industry. These methods have completely changed the way that trading is done, allowing for quicker and more effective trade execution. The ideas underlying HFT and algorithmic trading, as well as their advantages and disadvantages, will be discussed in this section, along with how AI is fostering innovation in these fields.

3.2.1 Gaining Knowledge about Algorithmic Trading

Trading in financial markets using computer algorithms is referred to as algorithmic trading, or "algo" trading. These algorithms are made to evaluate market data, spot trading opportunities, and carry out trades automatically in accordance with preset guidelines. Algorithmic trading aims to exploit market inefficiencies and eliminate human emotions and biases from the trading process.

The ability of algorithmic trading to execute trades quickly is one of its main benefits.

Algorithmic trading systems can process enormous volumes of market data in real-time and execute transactions in milliseconds by utilizing AI and cutting-edge computing capabilities. Because of their speed advantage, traders can profit from minute price differences as well as transient market fluctuations.

There are several sorts of algorithmic trading strategies, such as market-making, mean-reversion, statistical arbitrage, and trend-following. Different mathematical models and approaches are used by each strategy to find profitable trading chances. By adding machine learning algorithms that adjust and learn from market data to increase trading performance, these techniques can be further improved.

3.2.2 High-frequency trading's ascent

A subtype of algorithmic trading called high-frequency trading (HFT) is focused on carrying out a lot of deals at incredibly fast speeds. HFT firms evaluate market data in milliseconds and execute trades using complex algorithms and robust computing infrastructure.

Because HFT may profit from large trading volumes and tiny price differences, it has become more and more popular in recent years. HFT companies often use techniques like market-making, in which they constantly buy and sell shares to give the market liquidity. They benefit from both the volume of deals done and the bid-ask spread by doing this.

Low-latency trading infrastructure, such as fast data connections, co-location services, and sophisticated trading platforms, is essential to HFT's success. HFT companies can execute transactions more quickly than their rivals thanks to this technology, which gives them a big advantage in seizing market opportunities.

3.2.3 Advantages and Difficulties of HFT and Algorithmic Trading

HFT and algorithmic trading provide many advantages to market players. First off, by continuously supplying buy and sell orders, these strategies increase market liquidity by guaranteeing that a counterparty is always accessible for trades. All market players gain from this liquidity since it lowers transaction costs and raises price efficiency.

Second, by rapidly integrating new information into pricing, algorithmic trading, and HFT, we can improve market efficiency. These algorithms ensure that prices reflect the most recent information by assessing market data in real-time, allowing them to respond to news and events more quickly than human traders.

HFT and algorithmic trading, however, also present dangers and difficulties for the financial markets. A worry is the possibility of manipulating the market. The increasing sophistication of algorithmic trading systems poses a potential threat of price manipulation or artificial market fluctuations.

The growing intricacy and interdependence of financial markets is another obstacle. If not adequately handled, HFT and algorithmic trading can increase market volatility and cause flash crashes. The quick speed at which trades are completed has the potential to worsen market fluctuations and raise systemic risk.

Regulators have taken action to protect the integrity and stability of the financial markets after realizing these threats. In order to keep an eye on and manage algorithmic trading operations, rules including circuit breakers, position limits, and market surveillance systems have been implemented.

3.2.4   AI-Powered   Advances   in   HFT   and Algorithmic Trading

Significant advancements in HFT and algorithmic trading are being driven by AI. More advanced trading techniques that adjust and pick up knowledge from market data are being created using machine learning algorithms. Intricate correlations and patterns in market data that human traders would not see are recognized by these algorithms.

In order to acquire insights on investor behavior and market sentiment, natural language processing (NLP) techniques are also being used to evaluate news articles, sentiment on social media, and other textual data. AI-powered systems can make better trading judgments by utilizing these insights into their trading methods.

AI is also being utilized to enhance risk management in HFTs and algorithmic trading. More sophisticated AI algorithms are able to recognize possible dangers and weaknesses in trading strategies by analyzing past market data. These models can assist traders in better understanding the possible effects of their strategies and in making more informed decisions on risk management by simulating various market scenarios.

In conclusion, high-frequency trading and algorithmic trading are two effective uses of AI in the financial industry. These methods have completely changed the way that trading is done, allowing for quicker and more effective trade execution. Although they provide many advantages, they also come with hazards and difficulties that must be properly addressed. Algorithmic trading and HFT are expected to become even more important in the future of finance as AI technologies continue to progress.

3.3 AI-Powered Portfolio Optimization

One of the most important facets of investment management is portfolio optimization. It entails building an asset portfolio with the goal of maximizing returns and lowering risks. Historically, statistical analysis and mathematical models have been the foundation of portfolio optimization. However, new methods that can improve portfolio optimization's efficacy and efficiency have surfaced with the introduction of artificial intelligence (AI).

AI-powered portfolio optimization methods use machine learning and sophisticated algorithms to evaluate enormous volumes of data and pinpoint the best investment plans. Numerous aspects, such as past market data, economic indicators, corporate financials, and investor preferences, can be taken into account by these strategies. Investors can improve risk-adjusted returns and make more informed decisions by integrating AI into the portfolio optimization process.

3.3.1 Using Machine Learning to Optimize Portfolios

Algorithms for machine learning are essential to portfolio optimization. These algorithms are capable of analyzing previous market data and spotting trends and patterns that human analysts might miss. Machine learning models are able to forecast future market movements and modify portfolio allocations by leveraging historical market behavior.

A well-liked machine learning method for optimizing portfolios is "mean-variance optimization." This method takes into account the volatility and predicted returns of various assets in order to determine the ideal ratio of risk to return. For the purpose of estimating these characteristics and creating ideal portfolios, machine learning algorithms can examine volatility and historical return data.

A different machine learning method for portfolio optimization is called "reinforcement learning." To maximize a reward signal, reinforcement learning algorithms acquire knowledge through trial and error. By continuously modifying portfolio allocations in response to market feedback, these algorithms are able to develop optimal investment strategies in the context of portfolio optimization.

3.3.2 Optimization of Portfolios Using Genetic

Algorithms
Another effective approach for portfolio improvement is genetic algorithms. Genetic algorithms mimic the evolution of a population of viable solutions to determine the optimal portfolio allocation, drawing inspiration from the process of natural selection.

Genetic algorithms are used to optimize portfolios, and they begin with a population of randomly created portfolios. The performance of these portfolios is assessed, and the portfolios with the best results are chosen for replication. New portfolios are generated through crossover and mutation processes, and the cycle is perpetuated over several generations. The genetic algorithm gradually converges to the best portfolio allocation, which minimizes risks and maximizes returns.

The benefit of using genetic algorithms is that they can manage complex limitations and non-linear interactions between assets, as well as investigate a large range of potential solutions. Additionally, they have the flexibility to modify portfolio allocations in response to shifting market conditions.

3.3.3 Optimization of Portfolios Using Neural Networks

Portfolio optimization is another area in which neural networks—a class of machine learning model inspired by the human brain—have been used. Neural networks are an excellent tool for financial market analysis because they can recognize intricate patterns and relationships in data.

Neural networks can be trained to forecast asset returns in the context of portfolio optimization using a variety of input variables, including past prices, economic indicators, and news mood. Afterwards, the best possible portfolios that minimize risks and maximize returns can be created using these forecasts.

Additionally, hidden relationships can be found, and the interactions between various assets can be modeled using neural networks. Neural networks can improve the efficacy of portfolio optimization algorithms and produce predictions that are more accurate by incorporating these dependencies.

3.3.4 Benefits and Difficulties of Portfolio Optimization Driven by AI

AI-powered portfolio optimization has a number of benefits over conventional methods. First off, investors may make more prompt and knowledgeable selections because of AI techniques' ability to collect and evaluate enormous amounts of data far more quickly than humans can. Second, AI algorithms may find intricate links and patterns in data that human analysts might miss, which improves portfolio performance and makes predictions that are more accurate. Finally, the responsiveness and agility of investment strategies can be enhanced by AI-powered portfolio optimization, which can instantly modify portfolio allocations in response to shifting market conditions.

Nevertheless, portfolio optimization using AI is not without its difficulties. The requirement for trustworthy and high-quality data is one difficulty. For training and decision-making, AI models mostly depend on data, and any biases or mistakes in the data can provide less-than-ideal outcomes. The interpretability of AI models is another problem. Certain AI methods, such as neural networks, are sometimes referred to as "black boxes" since it can be difficult to comprehend how they make judgments. It may be challenging for investors to accept and validate the suggestions made by AI models due to their lack of interpretability.

The advantages of AI-powered portfolio optimization make it an attractive field for study and use in the financial sector, notwithstanding these difficulties. Investors may anticipate increasingly complex and precise portfolio optimization tactics that can increase investment performance and reduce risks as AI techniques continue to advance and improve.

3.4 AI and Risk Management in Investing
Investment strategies must include risk management, and the use of artificial intelligence (AI) in this process has completely changed how financial institutions handle this responsibility. Risk management systems with AI capabilities can analyze enormous volumes of data, spot trends, and make deft judgments instantly. The use of AI in risk management and how it affects investing choices are discussed in this section.

3.4.1 Artificial Intelligence for Hazard Evaluation
Conventional approaches to risk assessment in finance frequently depend on statistical models and historical data. Although these strategies have shown some degree of success, their flexibility in responding to quickly shifting market conditions is constrained. On the other hand, by utilizing cutting-edge algorithms and real-time data, AI has the potential to improve risk assessment.

Numerous data sources, including financial

statements, market news, sentiment on social media, and macroeconomic indicators, can be analyzed by AI algorithms. AI algorithms that process this data are able to recognize possible hazards and give investors timely advice. AI, for instance, can spot patterns in the market that could affect investment portfolios or anomalies in financial data that might point to fraud.

3.4.2 Using Machine Learning to Model Risk

In order to accurately estimate and predict risks, machine learning techniques are essential. These algorithms have the ability to learn from past data and spot trends that human analysts might miss. Machine learning models are capable of accurately predicting future dangers and identifying intricate linkages by evaluating big data.

The capacity of machine learning to adjust and learn from fresh data is one of its main benefits in risk management. Machine learning models have the ability to update their forecasts and modify risk management plans in response to changes in the market. Financial institutions are able to make well-informed investment decisions and remain ahead of developing dangers thanks to this flexibility.

3.4.3 Fraud Identification and Avoidance

The financial sector is very concerned about fraud, and sophisticated fraudulent operations are frequently difficult to detect using conventional methods of fraud detection. Advanced algorithms and machine learning approaches are employed by AI-powered fraud detection systems to identify abnormalities and patterns that might point to fraudulent activity.

Artificial intelligence (AI) systems can detect anomalous patterns and alert users to potentially fraudulent activity instantly by evaluating vast amounts of transactional data. Additionally, these systems are capable of learning from previous fraud cases and enhancing their capacity to recognize new fraud types over time. Financial institutions can prevent financial losses for their clients and save a substantial amount of money by taking a proactive approach to fraud detection.

3.4.4 Optimization of Portfolio Risk
One of the most important components of investment risk management is portfolio optimization. By taking into account a variety of risk factors and determining the ideal ratio of return to risk, investors can enhance their portfolios with the aid of AI approaches. Artificial intelligence (AI) algorithms can recommend portfolio allocations that optimize returns while limiting risk by examining past data, market patterns, and investor preferences.

AI-driven portfolio optimization algorithms can also take dynamic elements like shifting investor moods and market conditions into account. These systems have the ability to continuously watch the market and instantly modify portfolio allocations in response to shifting risk profiles. Investors can increase their overall investment performance and obtain better risk-adjusted returns by using this dynamic method for portfolio risk optimization.

3.4.5 Risk management and compliance with regulations

In the financial sector, regulatory compliance is a crucial component of risk management. Regulation violations can have a serious financial impact as well as harm to one's reputation. AI has the potential to be extremely helpful in guaranteeing regulatory compliance by automating compliance procedures and keeping an eye on transactions for possible infractions.

Compliance systems with AI capabilities are able to instantly identify any compliance concerns by analyzing vast amounts of data. Additionally, by analyzing previous compliance situations, these systems are able to modify their algorithms to meet evolving regulatory standards. Financial organizations can guarantee constant adherence to laws and lower the risk of human error by automating compliance activities.

In summary, AI has revolutionized the field of investment risk management. Artificial intelligence (AI) systems are capable of real-time data analysis, pattern recognition, and well-informed decision-making by utilizing sophisticated algorithms and machine learning methodologies. Artificial intelligence (AI) is completely changing how financial institutions manage risks and choose investments, from risk assessment and fraud detection to portfolio optimization and regulatory compliance. The possibility for better risk management in investing will only increase as AI develops.

PERSONALIZED FINANCIAL PLANNING

4.1 Financial Goal-Setting with AI

Achieving financial success requires setting financial goals. Historically, people have established these objectives by using their own discretion and expertise. But with the development of artificial intelligence (AI), people now have access to strong tools that can make it easier for them to set and meet their financial objectives.

AI-based financial goal setting analyzes a person's financial status, goals, and preferences using sophisticated algorithms and machine learning approaches. Artificial intelligence has the capability to offer tailored advice and approaches to assist people in achieving their financial objectives by utilizing extensive datasets and advanced models.

4.1.1 Comprehending Financial Objectives

It's critical to comprehend financial goals and their significance before delving into AI-based financial goal planning. Financial goals are particular targets that people set in order to attain their intended financial results. These objectives can differ greatly based on the circumstances and desires of the individual. Financial objectives that are frequently pursued include debt repayment, home ownership, retirement savings, and business startups.

Financial goal-setting is crucial for a number of reasons. First of all, goals provide people with a distinct sense of purpose and direction. They support people in setting priorities for their finances and making efficient resource allocations. Second, objectives provide a standard by which to gauge development and achievement. Setting measurable, precise goals allows people to monitor their progress and make necessary adjustments. Finally, having goals gives you a sense of success and motivation. Reaching financial objectives can provide one with a sense of contentment and happiness, as well as confidence.

4.1.2 AI's Function in Financial Goal-Setting

AI has the power to completely transform financial goal-setting by giving people individualized, data-driven insights. Conventional goal-setting techniques frequently depend on arbitrary guidelines or judgment calls. Conversely, artificial intelligence (AI) can use enormous data sets and complex algorithms to generate recommendations that are specifically customized for each person's set of circumstances.

AI is capable of analyzing a person's financial information, including their income, expenses, assets, and liabilities, to provide a thorough picture of their financial status. It can also consider external elements like economic statistics, market circumstances, and rates of inflation. AI can deliver more realistic and accurate financial future estimates for an individual by taking these things into account.

AI can also assist people in determining and prioritizing their financial objectives. AI may make recommendations about which objectives to prioritize and how best to distribute resources by examining a person's preferences, risk tolerance, and time horizon. For instance, depending on a person's unique situation, AI can recommend whether it is better to prioritize paying off debt or investing for retirement.

4.1.3 Advantages of AI-based Financial Goal Setting Compared to conventional techniques, AI-based financial goal-setting has a number of advantages. First of all, AI is able to offer customized advice based on each person's particular situation. Individual preferences, risk tolerance, and financial limits are all taken into consideration in this tailored approach, which produces more relevant and attainable goals.

Second, AI can give people a comprehensive picture of their financial status. Through simultaneous analysis of several financial factors, AI is able to detect possible conflicts or trade-offs between several objectives. AI, for instance, can assist people in comprehending the differences between investing in a retirement account and saving for a down payment on a home.

Thirdly, people can get immediate feedback and

direction from AI. AI is capable of adapting techniques and recommendations to individuals' progress toward their goals. With the help of this dynamic strategy, people are guaranteed to stay on course and make decisions based on the most recent facts.

Finally, AI can assist people in making the most of their financial resources. Artificial intelligence (AI) can recommend the most effective resource allocation to accomplish many goals at once by evaluating different situations and trade-offs. Through this optimization, people can increase their chances of success and make the most out of their financial resources.

4.1.4 Putting AI to Work in Financial Goal-Setting

People can use many platforms and solutions on the market to adopt AI-based financial goal planning. Usually, these apps ask users to enter their financial information and preferences, which are then examined by AI algorithms to generate customized tactics and recommendations.

People should think about things like data security, user friendliness, and supplier reputation when selecting an AI-based financial goal-setting tool. Making sure the tool fits a person's unique needs and objectives is also crucial.

After deciding on a tool, people can start the process of establishing their financial objectives.

Usually, this entails entering pertinent financial data, including assets, obligations, income, and spending. People might also be required to disclose information regarding their time horizon, risk tolerance, and preferences.

Once the required data has been entered, people can examine the suggestions and tactics that the AI tool has offered. It is imperative to meticulously contemplate these suggestions and evaluate their practicability and congruence with individual goals. People might also decide to speak with a financial expert to confirm the suggestions and get more advice.

After the methods and goals are decided upon, people can use the AI tool to monitor their progress. It is imperative to conduct periodic reviews and updates of the goals and strategies to guarantee their continued relevance and alignment with evolving circumstances.

4.1.5 AI-based Financial Goal Setting: Ethical Issues

Even though AI-based financial goal setting has many advantages, it's crucial to think about the moral ramifications of applying AI to one's own finances. Sharing private financial data with AI tools raises serious privacy and data security issues. To protect their data, people should make sure the technologies they use have strong security protections in place.

Important ethical considerations also include explainability and transparency. People ought to be fully aware of how AI algorithms generate suggestions and judgments. To help people make wise judgments, AI systems ought to include explanations and arguments for the suggestions they make.

People should also be conscious of the possibility of bias in AI programs. The historical data used to train AI algorithms may contain biases and inequalities. AI algorithms should be routinely assessed and audited to make sure that preexisting biases are not reinforced.

Finally, people need to exercise caution when depending too much on AI tools. AI should not take the place of human judgment and critical thinking, even though it can offer insightful analysis and helpful suggestions. Instead of depending exclusively on recommendations produced by AI, people should use AI technologies as a supplement to their own knowledge and experience.

To sum up, AI-based financial goal setting gives people a strong tool to create and meet their financial goals. Through the utilization of AI algorithms and data-driven insights, people can obtain customized advice and approaches that are suited to their specific situation. But when it comes to personal finance, it's critical to take into account the ethical ramifications and constraints of AI and use its capabilities to supplement human judgment.

4.2 Expense tracking and intelligent budgeting

An integral part of personal financial management is tracking expenses and creating an intelligent budget. Artificial intelligence (AI) has made it possible for people to access sophisticated tools and strategies that might help them better manage their finances. This section will examine how artificial intelligence (AI) is transforming budgeting and cost tracking to help people reach their financial objectives and make wise financial decisions.

4.2.1 Tools for Budgeting Driven by AI

Manual data entry and analysis is a common component of traditional budgeting techniques, which can be laborious and error-prone. On the other hand, machine learning algorithms are used by AI-powered budgeting applications to automate the process and give consumers real-time insights into their spending patterns. These systems have the ability to track income and costs, classify expenses, and offer tailored recommendations for optimal spending.

The capacity of AI-powered budgeting solutions to learn from user behavior and adjust to personal preferences is one of their main benefits. These tools help customers find areas where they can reduce expenditure or increase savings by examining past spending habits to find trends and anomalies. For instance, the tool can recommend cooking at home or looking into more reasonably priced dining options if a user routinely spends a large amount of their cash on eating out.

4.2.2 Monitoring and Analyzing Expenses

AI is also quite useful for tracking and analyzing expenses. Conventional approaches to tracking expenses typically entail entering costs by hand and utilizing spreadsheets or other tools for analysis. This procedure is automated by AI-powered expense monitoring systems, which automatically gather and classify costs from a variety of sources, including bank statements, credit card transactions, and receipts.

These technologies retrieve pertinent data from unstructured data sources, like bills and receipts, using natural language processing (NLP) approaches. AI systems that examine this data can give consumers comprehensive insights into their spending habits by pointing out areas in which they might be overspending or passing up chances to save money.

Personalized tips for optimizing spending can also be given to users by AI-powered expense tracking applications. For instance, the tool might uncover prospective subscription services that the user may no longer require or recommend ways to cut costs in particular categories depending on the user's spending patterns and financial objectives.

4.2.3 Financial Planning and Predictive Budgeting

By enabling predictive budgeting and financial planning, artificial intelligence (AI) may elevate budgeting and spending tracking to new heights. Artificial intelligence (AI) algorithms can estimate future income and expenses by evaluating past spending habits and financial data. This capability enables users to organize their finances more efficiently.

With the help of predictive budgeting tools, users can gain a forward-looking perspective of their financial status, enabling them to foresee future difficulties and proactively modify their spending patterns. For instance, the tool can recommend strategies to cut costs or look into new revenue streams if a user anticipates a decline in income in the upcoming months.

AI can help with long-term financial planning, including retirement planning, in addition to predictive budgeting. AI algorithms can offer individualized advice for retirement savings targets and investment strategies by evaluating a user's financial data and taking into account variables like inflation and investment returns.

4.2.4 Privacy and Security Concerns

Although there are many advantages to using AI-powered budgeting and cost monitoring software, security and privacy concerns must be taken into account. It is imperative for users to guarantee that the solutions they use comply with stringent data protection guidelines and utilize strong encryption methods to secure their financial data.

Users should also carefully read these tools' privacy rules to understand how their data will be shared and utilized. Selecting trustworthy suppliers who value user privacy and follow open data handling procedures is essential.

In summary

AI-powered intelligent budgeting and cost tracking are revolutionizing personal financial management. These technologies enable predictive budgeting and financial planning, automate expense tracking and analysis, and give customers real-time insights into their spending patterns. People may take charge of their finances, make wise financial decisions, and strive toward their financial objectives by utilizing AI. But while utilizing budgeting tools driven by AI, security and privacy concerns must be taken into account.

4.3 Retirement Planning Driven by AI

One of the most important areas of personal finance is retirement planning, which calls for thoughtful analysis and calculated choices. The development of artificial intelligence (AI) has given people access to effective tools and methods that can significantly improve the retirement planning process. This section will examine the different ways that artificial intelligence (AI) is transforming retirement planning and enabling people to make well-informed financial decisions.

4.3.1 Retirement Calculators Powered by AI

For many years, people have used retirement calculators to predict how much money they will need for a pleasant retirement. But conventional retirement calculators frequently ignore the complexity of unique financial situations and instead make oversimplified assumptions. Conversely, machine learning and sophisticated algorithms are used by AI-powered retirement calculators to produce more precise and individualized retirement estimates.

Numerous variables, including existing savings, projected income, expenses, inflation rates, and investment returns, are taken into account by these AI-powered calculators. These calculators can produce more accurate retirement forecasts and assist people in making well-informed decisions regarding their investment and savings plans by examining historical data and market trends.

4.3.2 Tailored Investment Suggestions

Selecting the best investment plan to meet long-term financial objectives is one of the main obstacles in retirement planning. AI-powered retirement planning systems are able to generate customized investment recommendations based on an individual's risk tolerance, retirement objectives, and financial profile.

These technologies can evaluate enormous volumes of financial data and pinpoint investment opportunities that fit a person's risk tolerance and retirement goals by utilizing machine learning algorithms. A variety of asset classes, including stocks, bonds, and real estate, may be suggested, depending on the particular requirements and preferences of the client.

4.3.3 Strategic Allocation of Assets

Since asset allocation establishes how investments

ZIED ILAHI

are distributed among various asset classes, it is a crucial component of retirement planning. Decisions about the distribution of assets were traditionally made using general principles or static rules of thumb. Nonetheless, asset allocation can be optimized by AI-powered retirement planning tools depending on user preferences and market conditions.

These technologies can dynamically modify asset allocation to maximize returns while limiting risk by examining past data and market patterns. They can also build a personalized asset allocation plan that fits a person's retirement objectives by taking into consideration variables like age, time horizon, and risk tolerance.

4.3.4 Evaluation of Longevity Risk

The term "longevity risk" describes the uncertainty surrounding an individual's predicted lifespan as well as the possible financial ramifications of exceeding expectations. AI-powered retirement planning tools examine a range of variables, including family history, lifestyle, and health, to determine the risk of a long life.

People can gain a better understanding of the possible effects of living longer than anticipated on their retirement resources by including longevity risk in their retirement predictions. With the use of this information, people can make better-informed choices about their investment and savings plans, including whether to buy long-term care insurance or annuities.

4.3.5 Ongoing Evaluation and Modifications

Retirement planning is a continuous process that needs to be regularly reviewed and adjusted, rather than being a one-time affair. AI-powered retirement planning solutions are able to monitor a person's retirement plan continuously and make adjustments in real time in response to shifting market conditions and individual circumstances.

These technologies can monitor the performance of investments, examine market patterns, and offer alerts and suggestions when changes are required. People can use AI to improve the trust they have in their retirement plan and make timely modifications to stay on track to reach their financial objectives.

4.3.6 Insights into Behavioral Finance

The study of psychological biases and emotions in relation to financial decision-making is known as behavioral finance. AI-driven retirement planning solutions can help people overcome common biases and make more logical and informed decisions by incorporating behavioral finance knowledge.

These technologies analyze financial data and human behavior patterns to find possible biases and offer tailored recommendations to lessen their effects. The tool can offer assistance to someone who tends to be excessively cautious or risk-taking in their investing selections, for instance, so they can make more sensible and well-rounded decisions.

To sum up, AI is transforming retirement planning by giving people the ability to make wise financial decisions by giving them access to sophisticated tools and strategies. AI-driven retirement planning solutions enable people to maximize their savings and investment strategies, from intelligent asset allocation and continuous monitoring to individualized retirement estimates. People can take proactive measures to safeguard their long-term financial well-being and feel more confident about their retirement plan by utilizing AI.

4.4 AI-Powered Financial Advice and Suggestions

People are continuously looking for trustworthy and individualized financial guidance in the quickly changing financial landscape in order to make wise financial decisions. The financial sector has seen a dramatic shift in the manner in which clients are given advice and suggestions with the introduction of artificial intelligence (AI). Large-scale data analysis, pattern recognition, and insight generation are all possible with AI-powered systems, which can assist people in making smarter financial decisions.

4.4.1 Financial Advisory Services Powered by AI
The creation of AI-driven financial advisory services is one of the main uses of AI in finance. These services use machine learning algorithms to assess a person's financial information, such as objectives, assets, income, and expenses, and then deliver recommendations and advice that are specific to that person. Artificial intelligence (AI)-powered solutions can provide individualized ways to maximize debt management, investments, and savings by learning about a person's financial goals and circumstances.

Financial advisory services powered by artificial intelligence (AI) can offer advice on managing debt, investing in a variety of asset classes, budgeting, and retirement savings. Sophisticated algorithms that consider variables like time horizon, market conditions, and risk tolerance behind these recommendations. Compared to conventional financial counselors, artificial intelligence (AI) can offer more relevant and accurate advice by taking a wide range of factors into account.

4.4.2 Advantages of Financial Advice Driven by AI
People can gain from using AI to provide financial advice in a number of ways. First of all, AI-powered systems have the capacity to instantly evaluate massive amounts of data, giving people access to current and pertinent advice. People can react swiftly to shifting market conditions and make

informed financial decisions thanks to this real-time analysis.

Second, financial advice powered by AI is incredibly tailored. When giving advice, traditional financial counselors frequently rely on broad guidelines and presumptions. On the other hand, AI systems are able to make recommendations that are specifically suited to each individual based on their goals, risk tolerance, and unique financial situation. This customized strategy can assist people in more successfully achieving their financial goals.

In addition, the expense of AI-driven financial advice is frequently lower than that of conventional financial advising services. The cost of using many AI-powered systems is far less than that of engaging a human financial counselor. Because of its affordability, financial advice is now available to a larger group of people, including those who might not have previously had access to it.

4.4.3 Obstacles and Things to Think About
Although there are many advantages to AI-driven financial advice, there are also issues and concerns that must be taken into account. The possibility of algorithmic bias is one of the main difficulties. Since AI systems are taught based on historical data, biases and inequalities may be present. Artificial intelligence-driven financial advice may unintentionally reinforce preexisting prejudices

and inequality in the financial system if these biases are not recognized and corrected.

The requirement for explainability and transparency presents another difficulty. Because AI algorithms can be intricate and complicated to comprehend, it can be difficult for users to put their trust and confidence in the recommendations made. It is imperative that AI systems give justifications for the suggestions they make and be open about how they make decisions. This openness can contribute to the development of confidence in and trust in AI-powered financial advice.

When employing AI to provide financial advice, privacy and security issues must also be taken into consideration. For AI systems to make tailored recommendations, access to a person's financial information is necessary. Strong security measures must be in place for these systems in order to safeguard sensitive personal data and guarantee data privacy.

4.4.4 AI-Powered Financial Advice's Future

AI-powered financial advice has a bright future ahead of it. We may anticipate more complex and precise recommendations as AI technologies develop. Artificial intelligence (AI) systems will improve in their ability to comprehend people's financial objectives and preferences, allowing them to offer increasingly relevant and tailored recommendations.

Furthermore, the user experience of AI-driven financial advice services will be improved by the integration of AI with other cutting-edge technologies like voice recognition and natural language processing. Seeking financial advice will become simpler and more natural when people can communicate with AI systems using natural language.

To sum up, AI-driven financial advice has the power to completely change how people handle their money. Through the use of AI technologies, people can get timely and individualized advice that might assist them in making wise financial decisions. However, to guarantee the responsible and moral application of AI in financial advice services, it is critical to address issues like algorithmic bias, transparency, and privacy. Financial guidance appears to have a bright future as AI develops further, enabling people to reach their financial objectives more confidently and effectively.

EFFICIENT DATA NAVIGATION IN FINANCE

5.1 Methods of Data Gathering and Preprocessing
The lifeblood of AI in finance is data. AI systems are unable to produce precise insights or reach well-informed conclusions in the absence of high-quality data. We will look at the methods in this section that the financial industry uses to gather and prepare data so that it is dependable, clean, and ready for analysis.

5.1.1 Information Gathering
The process of data analysis begins with data collection. Data in the financial industry can originate from a number of places, including the news media, regulatory agencies, financial institutions, and stock exchanges. The following are some typical methods for gathering data:

Web scraping: This is the process of obtaining information from websites. This method can be applied to the finance industry to gather news items, financial statements, stock prices, and other pertinent data. Large volumes of data can be effectively gathered from numerous sources using automated web scraping techniques.

Application Programming Interfaces, or APIs, give developers the ability to access and retrieve data from a variety of databases and financial platforms. APIs offer a standardized and organized method of data collection, which facilitates easier integration with AI systems. Real-time stock prices, historical market data, economic indicators, and more can all be obtained through financial APIs.

Data suppliers: The financial sector has specialized data providers who provide extensive databases for study. These suppliers gather and select information from multiple sources, guaranteeing its precision and dependability. Financial data suppliers include Thomson Reuters, FactSet, and Bloomberg.

Internal data sources: Internal databases are frequently found in financial organizations, and these databases hold important information for analysis. Customer transaction data, trade data, risk management data, and other types of data can be included in this. Gaining a competitive edge and exclusive insights might come from utilizing internal data sources.

5.1.2 Preparing the Data

To guarantee the quality and appropriateness of the data for analysis, preprocessing is required once it has been gathered. Data preparation entails arranging, cleaning, and altering the information. The following are some typical methods for preparing data in the finance industry:

Data cleaning is the process of eliminating or fixing any mistakes, discrepancies, or missing values from the dataset. This can involve managing outliers, eliminating duplicate entries, and calculating missing values using methods like mean or regression imputation.

Data transformation is the process of transforming data into a format that is appropriate for analysis. This can involve normalizing the data distribution, encoding and categorizing categories, and scaling numerical variables. Data transformation frequently makes use of methods including normalization, one-hot encoding, and logarithmic transformation.

Feature engineering: To enhance the functionality of AI models, feature engineering entails generating new features from the available data. This can be done in the field of finance by producing technical indicators, moving averages, and financial ratio calculations. To find pertinent features that can improve the models' predictive capacity, feature engineering calls for domain knowledge and experience.

Data integration: To produce a single, comprehensive dataset for analysis, data integration entails merging several datasets. This may entail compiling data at various granularities or combining information based on shared variables. Data integration can reveal hidden patterns and correlations and provide a comprehensive picture of the financial landscape.

5.1.3 Assurance of Data Quality

For precise analysis and trustworthy insights, it is imperative to ensure the quality of the data. Several methods are employed in finance to ensure the quality of data:

Verifying the correctness and integrity of the data is known as data validation. This can involve cross-referencing data with outside sources, detecting outliers, and validating data against predetermined guidelines or restrictions. Any flaws or inconsistencies in the dataset can be found and fixed with the use of data validation.

Data anonymization: sensitive data, including account details and personal information, must be safeguarded in the finance industry. Techniques for data anonymization, like encryption and masking, can be used to protect privacy and adhere to legal obligations.

Data governance is the process of managing and safeguarding data at every stage of its lifetime through the establishment of rules, guidelines, and controls. This entails establishing data ownership, guaranteeing data security, and upholding standards for data quality. Frameworks for data governance assist in preserving the accuracy and consistency of the data utilized in AI-driven finance.

To sum up, in order to fully utilize artificial intelligence in the banking industry, preprocessing and data collection methods are crucial. Financial institutions can get important insights, make wise decisions, and spur industry innovation by gathering high-quality data and using efficient preprocessing approaches.

5.2 Interpretation and Visualization of Data

An essential tool for comprehending and analyzing complex financial data is data visualization. Financial institutions are flooded with enormous volumes of data in the big data era, which needs to be properly evaluated and comprehended. Data visualization can help in this situation by giving financial professionals useful information and the ability to make defensible decisions.

5.2.1 Data Visualization's Significance in Finance
The graphical display of information and data is known as data visualization. It enables financial experts to visually represent complex data, which facilitates the understanding of links, patterns, and trends. Data visualization is crucial in the financial sector for a number of reasons, including:

Improved Understanding: Data visualization aids in the understanding of intricate financial linkages and concepts. Finance experts can spot patterns and trends in data that might not be obvious in raw form by using visual representations.

Better Decision Making: Finance professionals may make well-informed decisions by using data visualization to gain a clear knowledge of the facts. A comprehensive perspective is offered by visual representations of financial data, which facilitates improved analysis and decision-making.

Efficient Communication: Data visualization facilitates the communication of intricate financial information to stakeholders. Spreadsheets and written reports are typically less interesting and more difficult to read than visual representations.

Finding Anomalies: When analyzing financial data, data visualization can be used to spot outliers or anomalies. Finance experts can immediately identify anomalies that could need more research by displaying data.

Finding Opportunities: Financial data can contain hidden opportunities that data visualization can reveal. Finance professionals can spot possible market patterns or investment possibilities that might not be obvious from raw data by visualizing the data.

5.2.2 Financial Data Visualization Methods
For the purpose of data visualization in finance, there are numerous methods and resources accessible. Here are a few methods that are often

employed:

Line Charts: Trends throughout time are shown using line charts. When it comes to visualizing stock prices, market indexes, or any other type of time-series data, they are especially helpful.

Bar Charts: Bar charts are used for group or category comparisons. They are frequently used to display portfolio performance, market share information, and financial statements.

Pie Charts: Proportions and percentages are shown using pie charts. They are frequently employed to display market share or asset allocation data.

Scatter Plots: Scatter plots are a useful tool for illustrating how two variables relate to one another. They are frequently used in the finance industry to find outliers or assess the association between various financial instruments.

Heat Maps: By utilizing colors to indicate values, heat maps are used to visualize huge datasets. In the finance industry, they are frequently employed to examine portfolio performance, risk exposure, and market volatility.

Treemaps: Hierarchical data can be seen using treemaps. In finance, they are frequently used to illustrate market capitalization or portfolio makeup.

Gantt charts are a useful tool for visualizing dependencies and project timeframes. In finance, they are frequently used to monitor and oversee project progress.

5.2.3 Financial Data Visualization Tools

For data visualization in finance, there are several tools at one's disposal. Here are a few well-known ones:

Tableau: Finance professionals may create interactive dashboards and reports with Tableau, a powerful tool for data visualization. It facilitates integration with several data sources and provides an extensive array of display choices.

Power BI: Microsoft's business analytics product allows financial professionals to produce interactive reports and visualizations. It facilitates interaction with Microsoft Excel and other data sources and has an easy-to-use interface.

Python is a well-liked programming language for visualizing and analyzing data. It provides a number of libraries that provide powerful visualization creation tools, like Matplotlib and Seaborn.

R: R is a popular computer language for data visualization and statistical research. It provides a number of programs with sophisticated visualization features, including ggplot2 and plotly.

Excel: Excel is a popular spreadsheet program with some basic features for visualizing data. It works well for brief analyses and straightforward visualizations.

5.2.4 Fintech Data Visualization Best Practices
Adhering to established standards is crucial for ensuring efficient data visualization in the finance industry. Here are some crucial things to remember:

Simplicity: Avoid clutter and maintain basic visualizations. To improve readability, use simple design components, appropriate colors, and labels that are easy to read.

Relevance: Minimize extraneous details and concentrate on the most pertinent information. Emphasize the most important patterns and insights that are necessary for making decisions.

Consistency: Keep dashboards and reports' visuals consistent with one another. To produce a unified visual experience, use consistent typefaces, colors, and design components.

Interactivity: To encourage users to delve further into the data, including interactive features like tooltips and filters. Deeper investigation is made easier, and user engagement is increased by interactive visuals.

Accessibility: Make certain that all users, including those who are visually impaired, can access the visualizations. Make use of suitable color contrasts and give visual elements alternate text descriptions.

Contextualization: To facilitate understanding, give background information and justifications for visual aids. Add pertinent headings, annotations, and captions to help users comprehend the data.

Finance professionals can effectively use data visualization to get insightful information and make well-informed decisions by adhering to these best practices.

To sum up, data visualization is an effective method for deciphering intricate financial data. It makes decisions better, promotes better understanding, and makes effective communication easier. Finance professionals may fully realize the potential of data visualization in the AI-driven financial revolution by utilizing the right methodologies and tools.

5.3 Financial Data: Natural Language Processing

A subfield of artificial intelligence called natural language processing (NLP) is concerned with how computers and human language interact. It makes it possible for computers to produce, comprehend, and interpret human language, which makes it possible to extract insightful information from unstructured textual data. NLP is essential to the analysis and processing of large volumes of financial data in the finance domain. Examples of this type of data include news articles, research studies, social media posts, and regulatory filings.

5.3.1 Emotional Reporting for Monetary News

Sentiment analysis, or figuring out the sentiment or emotional tone conveyed in textual data, is one of the main uses of natural language processing (NLP) in the finance industry. Sentiment research is especially helpful when examining social media posts and financial news items to determine how investors and the market feel about particular businesses, industries, or financial products.

Financial analysts and traders can obtain significant insights into market sentiment and make better-informed investment decisions by utilizing natural language processing (NLP) techniques, such as text classification and sentiment scoring. Opinion analysis, for instance, can point to a possible purchasing opportunity if it shows a favorable opinion for a certain stock. On the other hand, a negative mood can point to a potential selling opportunity or the necessity for prudence.

5.3.2 Financial Entities' Named Entity Recognition

A further significant NLP method in the banking industry is named entity recognition (NER). NER is the process of locating and categorizing named entities—such as the names of businesses, individuals, locations, and financial terms—within a given text. NER can be used to extract important information from textual data sources such as research reports, news stories, and other sources in the financial realm.

Through the automatic identification and classification of financial institutions, NER facilitates the efficient collection of pertinent data and the acquisition of insights into industry dynamics, corporate performance, and market trends for financial analysts and researchers. To help analysts conduct quantitative research more effectively, NER can be used, for instance, to extract important financial indicators from firm financial statements, such as revenue, profit, and market capitalization.

5.3.3 Financial Research Topic Modeling

Using the potent NLP approach of topic modeling, one can find hidden themes or subjects in a set of documents. Topic modeling can be used to determine and examine the primary subjects covered in research reports, regulatory filings, and other textual data sources in the context of financial research.

Financial scholars can find the underlying themes and trends in a sizable corpus of financial documents by using topic modeling approaches like Latent Dirichlet Allocation (LDA). They might use this to recognize new trends in the market, comprehend the workings of the sector, and come up with fresh investment concepts. By revealing the primary subjects covered in research reports on a certain industry, for instance, topic modeling helps analysts better comprehend the market and make more intelligent investment choices.

5.3.4 Financial Reports Text Synopsis

An NLP technique called text summarizing involves creating a succinct synopsis of a given text. Text summarization can be used to automatically create executive summaries or key highlights from long research reports, earnings transcripts, and other financial documents in the context of financial reports.

Financial analysts and investors who need to swiftly assimilate the key conclusions and insights from a huge volume of textual data might save time and effort by using natural language processing (NLP) algorithms to automatically summarize financial reports. For portfolio managers, who must stay current on news and research to make wise investment decisions, this can be very helpful.

5.3.5 Financial FAQ Question-Answering Systems

In the financial sector, question-answering (QA)

systems driven by natural language processing (NLP) approaches are gaining traction. Based on data from databases, financial papers, and other textual data sources, these systems let users ask queries in plain language and obtain precise and pertinent responses.

QA systems can respond quickly and accurately to commonly requested inquiries regarding financial products, investment strategies, regulatory requirements, and other financial issues by utilizing natural language processing (NLP) algorithms. This can simplify the information-access process for both professionals and regular investors, increase investor education, and improve customer service in financial institutions.

To sum up, NLP is an effective technique for examining and deriving insights from financial data. Financial experts can obtain a more profound comprehension of market trends, corporate performance, and industry dynamics by utilizing natural language processing (NLP) techniques such as sentiment analysis, named entity recognition, topic modeling, text summarization, and question-answering systems. In the financial sector, this may result in better risk management, better investment choices, and higher levels of client service. It is anticipated that NLP's financial applications will rise as it develops, creating new avenues for innovation and expansion in the AI-driven financial revolution.

5.4 Financial Data Mining and Knowledge Discovery

In the banking sector, knowledge discovery and data mining are essential tools that help financial firms glean insightful information from massive data sets. The development of artificial intelligence (AI) has increased the strength and effectiveness of these procedures. This section will examine the advantages artificial intelligence (AI) offers the banking sector as well as how it is transforming data mining and knowledge discovery in the sector.

5.4.1 AI-driven Data Mining Methodologies

Finding patterns, connections, and trends in huge databases is a process known as data mining. This task used to take a lot of human labor and knowledge. But as AI has developed, data mining has gotten more precise and automated.

Machine learning is one of the main AI methods used in data mining. Massive amounts of financial data can be analyzed by machine learning algorithms, which can also spot trends that people would miss. By utilizing past data, these algorithms are able to forecast and suggest future financial moves.

Deep learning is another AI method used in data mining. Neural networks and other deep learning algorithms are capable of processing large amounts of financial data and extracting insightful information. These algorithms can find hidden patterns and correlations in data by autonomously learning hierarchical representations.

5.4.2 Financial Knowledge Discovery

The process of gleaning useful information from financial data is known as knowledge discovery in the finance industry. Utilizing this information will help you reduce risks, create investing strategies, and make well-informed decisions. Because AI makes it possible to analyze financial data more accurately and efficiently, it has greatly improved the process of knowledge discovery.

Knowledge discovery heavily relies on the AI technique of natural language processing (NLP). Unstructured financial text data, including news stories, research reports, and social media posts, can be analyzed and interpreted by NLP algorithms. Financial institutions can obtain important insights into market patterns, investor moods, and emerging threats by extracting pertinent information from various sources.

Anomaly detection is another AI method used in knowledge discovery. Algorithms for detecting anomalies can spot odd trends or outliers in financial data. This can be especially helpful in identifying instances of fraud, manipulation of the market, or unusual trading patterns.

Early detection of anomalies allows financial organizations to take the necessary precautions to reduce risks and safeguard their assets.

5.4.3 AI's advantages for knowledge discovery and data mining

The banking sector gains from the application of AI to data mining and knowledge discovery in a number of ways.

Enhanced Accuracy: AI systems are capable of accurately analyzing vast amounts of financial data, which lowers the possibility of biases and mistakes made by humans.

Enhanced Efficiency: Large volumes of data can be processed by AI-powered data mining techniques in a fraction of the time that a human would need to complete the same operation. Financial institutions are able to make judgments more quickly and intelligently as a result.

Finding Hidden Insights: Artificial intelligence (AI) systems have the ability to find hidden links and patterns in financial data that human analysts might miss. This may result in the identification of fresh investment prospects or the prompt identification of possible hazards.

Automation of Repetitive Processes: AI can automate data mining processes that are repetitive, freeing up human analysts to concentrate on more strategic and complicated duties.

Real-time Analysis: Financial institutions are able to react swiftly to market fluctuations and make informed judgments because AI algorithms are capable of analyzing financial data in real-time.

5.4.4 Obstacles and Things to Think About
While data mining and knowledge discovery in finance greatly benefit from AI, there are several issues and concerns that must be taken into account as well:

Data Quality and Bias: The representativeness and quality of the training data greatly influence the accuracy and dependability of AI algorithms. Financial institutions are required to guarantee the accuracy, timeliness, and lack of bias in the data they utilize for analysis.

Interpretability: AI algorithms have the potential to be complicated and challenging to understand, particularly deep learning models. To maintain regulatory compliance and transparency, financial institutions must create ways to justify the decisions that AI algorithms make.

Privacy and Security: Access to sensitive financial data is necessary for the application of AI in data mining and knowledge discovery. Strong security measures must be put in place by financial institutions to safeguard the confidentiality and privacy of this data.

Ethical Considerations: AI algorithms ought to be created and applied morally. Financial institutions must make sure that knowledge discovery and data mining procedures driven by AI adhere to moral and regulatory requirements and do not produce unfair or discriminatory activities.

In summary

AI has completely changed the financial industry's use of data mining and knowledge discovery, allowing organizations to glean insightful information from massive volumes of data. AI techniques such as machine learning, deep learning, natural language processing, and anomaly detection have revolutionized these operations. AI may help with data mining and knowledge discovery in a number of ways, including real-time analysis, increased productivity, automated repetitive operations, and the finding of hidden ideas. To guarantee the ethical and responsible application of AI in finance, however, issues including data quality and bias, interpretability, privacy and security, and ethical considerations must be resolved.

ACCESSING INACCESSIBLE FINANCIAL INSIGHTS

6.1 AI for Loan Approval and Credit Scoring

Credit scoring and loan approval are crucial procedures in the financial industry that establish a person's or company's eligibility for credit. These procedures have historically relied significantly on manual assessment and analysis, making them laborious and subjective. However, credit score and loan acceptance have undergone a revolution with the introduction of artificial intelligence (AI), becoming more effective, accurate, and inclusive.

Large data sets can be analyzed by AI algorithms, and they can spot correlations and patterns that human analysts would miss. This makes it possible for financial companies to decide on credit score and loan acceptance with greater knowledge. Lenders may cut expenses, expedite procedures, and give quicker, more accurate credit decisions by utilizing AI.

6.1.1 Credit Scoring Assisted by AI

The method of determining an individual's or company's creditworthiness based on their financial history—which includes things like payment history, amount of outstanding debt, and credit utilization—is known as credit scoring. Credit scoring methods have typically depended on a small number of criteria and human opinion. But by utilizing cutting-edge machine learning techniques and a larger variety of data sources, AI has the ability to improve credit scoring algorithms.

In addition to traditional credit data, AI-powered credit scoring models can examine data from other sources, including social media posts, online purchasing habits, and even the usage patterns of smartphones. Artificial intelligence algorithms have the capacity to generate a more thorough and precise evaluation of a person's creditworthiness by taking into account a wider variety of facts. Those with a short credit history or those who were not included in the typical credit scoring algorithms may find this to be especially helpful.

AI algorithms also have the capacity to continuously learn from and adjust to shifting customer behavior and market situations. This implies that real-time updates to credit scoring algorithms enable lenders to make more precise and current lending choices. Financial organizations can increase their capacity for risk assessment and make better loan decisions by utilizing AI.

6.1.2 Loan Approval using AI

The process through which lenders evaluate borrowers' creditworthiness and determine whether to approve a loan for them is known as loan approval. Loan approval procedures have historically been laborious and manual, including a lot of paperwork and human involvement. However, the loan approval process might be streamlined and automated by AI, which would make it quicker, more effective, and less prone to human error.

Artificial intelligence (AI) algorithms are capable of evaluating vast amounts of data, such as tax returns, bank statements, and other pertinent records, in order to evaluate borrowers' creditworthiness. Artificial intelligence (AI) can drastically cut down on the time and effort needed for loan approval by automating the review of these documents. This facilitates quicker loan application processing for lenders and quicker credit availability for customers.

AI algorithms can also find correlations and patterns in loan data that human analysts might miss. In order to identify possible hazards and make more accurate loan decisions, this can assist lenders. For instance, by examining behavioral patterns and spotting discrepancies in the information that borrowers submit, artificial intelligence systems are able to identify fraudulent loan applications.

AI-driven loan approval can increase inclusion in the lending process in addition to efficiency and accuracy. Artificial intelligence (AI) algorithms have the capability to evaluate the creditworthiness of people without a traditional credit history by utilizing sophisticated machine learning techniques and other data sources. This can encourage financial inclusion and increase loan availability for underprivileged groups.

6.1.3 AI's advantages and difficulties in credit scoring and loan approval

Lenders and borrowers can reap numerous advantages from the integration of AI in credit assessment and loan approval processes. Among the main advantages are:

Increased accuracy: AI systems are able to examine vast amounts of data and spot correlations and patterns that human analysts would miss. Decisions about loan acceptance and credit score may become more accurate as a result.

Faster processing: AI can expedite and automate loan approval and credit scoring procedures, saving lenders time and effort when determining creditworthiness. Borrowers can now obtain financing more rapidly as a result.

Improved inclusivity: AI systems are able to evaluate the creditworthiness of people who do not have a typical credit history by using sophisticated machine learning techniques and alternative data sources. This may facilitate underprivileged groups' increased access to loans.

The use of AI in credit rating and loan approval has many advantages, but there are drawbacks as well. Among these difficulties are:

Data security and privacy: In order for AI algorithms to provide reliable credit judgments, they need access to vast amounts of data. Data security and privacy are put at risk because private financial information must be shielded from unwanted access.

Discrimination and bias: The quality of AI systems depends on the data they are trained on. When it comes to credit score and loan acceptance decisions, AI systems may reinforce prejudices found in the training data if these patterns are discriminatory. To prevent discriminating results, it is essential to make sure AI algorithms are trained on a variety of objective and varied data sets.

Explainability and transparency: AI systems are capable of being intricate and challenging to understand. Because of this lack of clarity and explainability, it may be difficult for borrowers to comprehend the variables influencing their credit decisions. It is imperative to create AI models that are visible and comprehensible in order to foster confidence and guarantee responsibility.

In conclusion, AI has the power to completely transform the banking industry's loan approval and credit rating systems. Lenders may increase the precision, effectiveness, and inclusivity of their lending decisions by utilizing AI algorithms. But in order to guarantee that an AI-driven credit score and loan approval are equitable, open, and reliable, it is crucial to address the issues around AI adoption, such as data privacy, bias, and explainability.

6.2 AI-Based Fraud Detection and Prevention

In the financial sector, fraud is a major issue that costs people and companies billions of dollars annually. Conventional approaches to fraud detection and prevention frequently aren't able to keep up with the constantly changing strategies that scammers use. However, there is new hope in the fight against fraud thanks to the development of artificial intelligence (AI) technologies. Systems driven by AI have the ability to identify and stop fraudulent activity more accurately and effectively than in the past.

6.2.1 AI's Function in Fraud Detection

Artificial intelligence (AI) algorithms are able to evaluate enormous volumes of data in real-time, which allows them to spot patterns and anomalies that can point to fraud. AI systems may continuously learn from fresh data by utilizing machine learning techniques, and they can then modify their fraud detection models accordingly. This enables them to identify fraudulent behaviors that were previously undiscovered and to stay ahead of new fraud trends.

Processing both organized and unstructured data is one of AI's main advantages in fraud detection. Unstructured data, such as written documents or social media posts, might include important information regarding possible fraud, but traditional rule-based systems frequently have trouble handling it. This unstructured data can be analyzed by AI-powered natural language processing (NLP) algorithms, which can also extract pertinent insights and improve overall fraud detection skills.

6.2.2 Using Machine Learning to Identify Fraud

By allowing AI systems to learn from historical data and recognize patterns that are suggestive of fraudulent activity, machine learning algorithms are essential to the identification of fraud. These algorithms can learn the traits of fraudulent activity by being trained on big datasets that include both fraudulent and lawful transactions.

It is possible to create prediction models with supervised machine learning algorithms that give each transaction a probability score that indicates how likely it is to be fraudulent. Labeled data, in which every transaction is classified as either genuine or fraudulent, can be used to train these models. These labeled instances teach the algorithm, which uses the patterns it has discovered to classify fresh transactions.

On the other hand, anomalies in the data can be found using unsupervised machine learning techniques. These algorithms concentrate on recognizing patterns that drastically depart from the norm, and they do not require labeled data. These algorithms can assist in identifying possible fraud cases by detecting transactions that have odd behavior.

6.2.3 Using Deep Learning to Identify Fraud

The capacity of deep learning, a kind of machine learning, to handle and interpret complicated data has drawn a lot of interest recently. Neural networks and other deep learning techniques are particularly useful for problems involving large and varied datasets that entail fraud detection.

Deep learning's capacity to automatically extract pertinent features from the data is one of its main advantages. This removes the requirement for manual feature engineering, in which subject matter experts must locate and choose the features most pertinent to the fraud detection assignment. These characteristics can be directly learned by deep learning algorithms from the raw data, enabling more reliable and accurate fraud detection models.

To improve fraud detection capabilities, deep learning algorithms can be coupled with other AI methods like natural language processing. Deep learning algorithms can detect suspicious patterns or keywords that can point to fraudulent activity by examining text data, such as emails or chat logs.

6.2.4 AI-powered real-time fraud detection

Real-time operation is one of the main benefits of AI-powered fraud detection systems.

Conventional techniques for detecting fraud frequently depend on batch processing, in which data is examined on a regular basis, delaying the discovery and prevention of fraud. On the other hand, the real-time data analysis capabilities of AI algorithms enable prompt action to be taken in the event that fraudulent activity is discovered.

AI-powered real-time fraud detection entails ongoing transaction monitoring and prompt detection of any suspicious trends or abnormalities. AI systems are able to promptly identify potentially fraudulent behaviors by examining each transaction as it happens. This allows them to set off automated reactions or alarms to stop additional harm from happening.

6.2.5: Using AI to Improve Fraud Prevention
AI has a significant role not only in fraud detection but also in fraud prevention. Artificial intelligence (AI) technologies can assist financial institutions in proactively implementing fraud prevention measures by evaluating historical data and spotting patterns that point to fraudulent behavior.

AI systems, for instance, are able to examine consumer behavior and spot odd trends that might point to identity theft or account takeover. Financial institutions can take quick action to confirm the customer's identification and stop illegal access to accounts by reporting these questionable behaviors.

AI may also be used to improve authentication procedures, which will make it harder for criminals to obtain private data without authorization. Artificial intelligence (AI) algorithms can assess whether a transaction is likely to be fraudulent or legitimate by examining a variety of characteristics, including user behavior, device information, and biometric data. This capability enables more secure authentication procedures.

6.2.6 AI-powered Fraud Detection: Ethical Considerations

Even though fraud detection systems driven by AI have many advantages, there are ethical issues that must be taken into account. When AI algorithms are used for fraud detection, there is a chance that they will produce false positives— the flagging of normal transactions as fraudulent. Customers may experience inconvenience as a result, and their confidence in financial institutions may be eroded.

Financial institutions must find a balance between fraud detection and client satisfaction. For the purpose of reducing false positives and making sure that valid transactions are not mistakenly reported as fraudulent, AI algorithms should be constantly reviewed and improved.

Concerns about data security and privacy are also raised by the application of AI in fraud detection. Financial institutions are responsible for making sure that consumer data is managed safely and in accordance with applicable laws. Sustaining customer trust and confidence in the use of AI algorithms also requires responsibility and transparency.

In summary, artificial intelligence (AI) has the power to completely transform fraud detection and prevention in the financial sector. AI-powered systems can evaluate enormous volumes of data in real-time, spot patterns suggestive of fraudulent activity, and take quick action to stop additional harm by utilizing machine learning and deep learning algorithms. To guarantee that the advantages of AI-powered fraud detection are matched with customer experience and data privacy, ethical considerations must be made.

6.3 AI for Adherence to Regulations

Ensuring that financial institutions comply with laws, rules, and industry standards is a crucial element of the financial business. Serious fines, harm to one's reputation, and even legal repercussions may arise from breaking these rules. Conventional compliance techniques are becoming insufficient due to the ever-changing financial landscape and the ever-increasing complexity of rules. Artificial intelligence (AI) can help with this by providing creative ways to improve regulatory compliance procedures.

6.3.1 Setting Up Automated Compliance Tracking
The requirement to continuously monitor enormous volumes of data in order to spot possible infractions is one of the major obstacles to regulatory compliance. By using machine learning algorithms to instantly examine massive amounts of data, artificial intelligence (AI) can automate this procedure. Artificial intelligence (AI) models can be trained on past compliance data to detect patterns and anomalies that might point to non-compliance. This makes it possible for financial institutions to identify any infractions more quickly and take proactive steps to resolve them.

6.3.2 Improving Procedures for Knowing Your Customer (KYC)
Financial organizations rely heavily on KYC procedures to confirm the legitimacy of their clients and evaluate the risks involved in their business dealings. Traditional KYC procedures, however, might demand a lot of time and resources. By automating the gathering and processing of consumer data, AI can optimize

these procedures. Machine learning algorithms are capable of determining a customer's risk profile by analyzing their transaction history and other data points, while natural language processing (NLP) techniques can be used to extract pertinent information from documents like utility bills and passports. This raises the accuracy of risk evaluations while simultaneously increasing the efficiency of KYC procedures.

6.3.3 Fraud Identification and Avoidance

For financial organizations as well as their clients, financial fraud is a serious risk. By examining vast amounts of transactional data and seeing suspicious trends, artificial intelligence (AI) can be extremely helpful in discovering and stopping fraud. Algorithms for machine learning can be trained on past fraud instances to find common fraud indications and instantly flag transactions that might be fraudulent. Furthermore, anomaly detection methods driven by AI can spot odd behavior that might point to fraud. Financial organizations can reduce losses and safeguard the assets of their clients by utilizing AI in fraud detection and prevention.

6.3.4 Keeping an eye on and reporting questionable activity

Financial institutions have an obligation to keep an eye on and report any suspicious activity that might point to money laundering, financing of terrorism, or other illegal activity. By automating transaction monitoring and spotting questionable patterns, AI can help with this process. Artificial intelligence (AI) systems can identify anomalous transactional behavior and produce alerts for additional inquiry by evaluating vast amounts of transactional data. This guarantees adherence to regulatory reporting obligations while simultaneously increasing the effectiveness of monitoring procedures.

6.3.5 Simplifying the Documentation of Compliance

A vital component of regulatory compliance is compliance documentation, which mandates that financial institutions keep thorough records of all of their compliance-related actions. By automating the creation and administration of compliance documentation, AI can expedite this procedure. Using preset templates and data inputs, natural language generation (NLG) techniques can be utilized to automatically develop policies, procedures, and compliance reports. In addition to saving time and money, this guarantees accuracy and consistency in compliance documents.

6.3.6 Scenario analysis and risk assessment

A crucial component of regulatory compliance is risk assessment, which helps financial organizations recognize and reduce possible hazards. By using machine learning algorithms to evaluate historical data and pinpoint risk variables, artificial intelligence (AI) can improve risk assessment procedures. Artificial intelligence (AI) models can be trained on historical risk data to learn how to recognize patterns and correlations that might point to possible hazards. AI may also help with scenario analysis by modeling different risk scenarios and evaluating how they might affect a financial organization. As a result, financial institutions are better equipped to make wise decisions and create strategies for reducing risk.

In conclusion, artificial intelligence (AI) has the power to completely transform regulatory compliance in the financial industry. Artificial intelligence (AI) can greatly increase the efficacy and efficiency of regulatory compliance processes by automating compliance monitoring, improving KYC procedures, identifying and preventing fraud, tracking and reporting suspicious activity, streamlining compliance documentation, and enabling risk assessment and scenario analysis. To guarantee openness, responsibility, and equity, it is crucial to remember that the application of AI in regulatory compliance needs to be supported by strong governance frameworks and moral concerns.

6.4 Financial Risk Assessment Driven by AI

One of the most important aspects of the financial sector is financial risk assessment. It entails assessing the possible risks connected to different financial operations, including lending, investments, and credit ratings. Financial risk assessment has typically depended on subjective assessment and laborious analysis. But the process has changed with the introduction of artificial intelligence (AI), making risk assessment more precise and effective.

6.4.1 Using Machine Learning to Assess Risk

In assessing financial risk, machine learning algorithms have proven to be incredibly successful. Large volumes of historical data can be analyzed by these algorithms to find patterns and trends that might point to possible dangers. Machine learning algorithms can identify risk characteristics and forecast future dangers by being trained on historical data.

Logistic regression is a well-liked machine learning method in financial risk assessment. This method uses a set of input variables to forecast the likelihood that an event will occur. Logistic regression is a useful tool in financial risk assessment as it may be used to forecast loan default rates and the chance of fraudulent transactions.

Decision trees are another effective machine-learning method for risk assessment. Decision trees are hierarchical models that divide data recursively according to several criteria in order to generate predictions. These models can shed light on the variables that contribute to financial risks and are especially helpful in determining intricate correlations between variables.

6.4.2 Using Neural Networks to Assess Risk

Inspired by the structure of the human brain, neural networks have become increasingly popular due to their capacity to resolve challenging issues. Neural networks can be used to examine large and diverse datasets in financial risk assessment in order to find hidden patterns and relationships.

The feedforward neural network is one kind of neural network that is frequently used in risk assessment. Each node in this network performs a mathematical operation on its inputs, and it is made up of several layers of interconnected nodes. The network may learn to forecast future risks based on the input variables by being trained on past data.

Another kind of neural network that can be applied to risk assessment is the recurrent neural network (RNN). Because RNNs are built to handle sequential data, they are an excellent choice for time series data analysis in the financial industry. RNNs are capable of accurately predicting and capturing the dynamics of financial risks by taking into account the temporal dependencies present in the data.

6.4.3 Using Natural Language Processing for Hazard Evaluation

Financial risk assessment can also benefit from the application of natural language processing (NLP) tools, especially when examining textual data like news articles, social media posts, and financial reports. NLP algorithms are able to evaluate the possible hazards connected to specific financial activity by extracting pertinent information from unstructured text.

An NLP method that is frequently employed in risk assessment is sentiment analysis. It entails examining the mood reflected in textual data to determine how the market views particular financial products or occurrences. Financial firms can spot possible hazards and modify their plans by keeping an eye on mood.

An additional NLP method that can be helpful in risk assessment is named entity recognition. It entails locating and categorizing identified entities in textual data, including persons, companies, and locations. Financial institutions can learn more about the possible hazards connected to particular entities by examining the relationships between these organizations.

6.4.4 Using Reinforcement Learning to assess risk AI's reinforcement learning field focuses on educating agents to make choices in uncertain situations. Although it is not as widely applied in financial risk assessment as other methods, this approach has the power to completely transform the industry.

Reinforcement learning is a useful tool for managing portfolio risks and optimizing investment strategies in the context of risk assessment. Reinforcement learning algorithms can learn to negotiate complex risk-reward trade-offs and make optimal judgments by teaching an agent to make decisions based on rewards and penalties and modeling the financial market as an environment.

It is crucial to remember that the field of reinforcement learning for risk assessment is still in its infancy and that there are obstacles to be addressed, including the requirement for a large amount of training data and the possibility of model instability. However, as this field of study develops, reinforcement learning may prove to be a formidable instrument for evaluating financial risk.

In summary

Financial institutions' assessment and management of risks are being revolutionized by AI-powered financial risk assessment. More precise and effective risk assessment is made possible by machine learning, neural networks, natural language processing, and reinforcement learning approaches. This promotes more informed decision-making and increased financial stability. We may anticipate more developments in risk assessment as AI progresses, which will influence how the financial sector develops in the future.

MARKETING STRATEGY FOR AI IN FINANCE

7.1 Digital Marketing and Online Advertising

Online advertising and digital marketing are now indispensable instruments for promoting goods and services in the current digital era. The financial industry is no different, aiming to use AI's capabilities to expand its online presence and connect with more people. The several approaches and methods that can be used to successfully promote AI-driven financial services and solutions will be discussed in this section.

7.1.1 Realizing the Significance of Internet Promotion

Compared to traditional types of advertising, online advertising has many advantages. Financial institutions can use it to track the success of their campaigns, target particular demographics, and instantly improve their marketing efforts. Financial institutions can construct more individualized and targeted advertising campaigns by using AI to assist them in obtaining insightful data about consumer behavior, interests, and trends.

7.1.2 AI-Powered Targeted Advertising

By evaluating enormous volumes of data and seeing patterns and trends, artificial intelligence (AI) can be extremely helpful in optimizing online advertising efforts. Financial institutions can tailor their marketing to certain audiences based on variables like age, region, income level, and interests by utilizing AI algorithms. This degree of accuracy guarantees that the appropriate message reaches the appropriate audience at the appropriate moment, boosting conversion rates and optimizing return on investment.

7.1.3 Using Marketing Insights from Data Analytics

Data analytics is a potent instrument that can offer insightful information on the interests and behaviors of consumers. Financial institutions can learn more about their target market by examining data gathered from multiple sources, including social media platforms, website analytics, and customer reviews. AI-powered data analytics technologies can assist in finding correlations, trends, and patterns that can help guide marketing plans and enhance consumer interaction.

7.1.4 Digital Marketing: Customization and Personalization

Customizing and personalizing marketing messaging is one of AI's main benefits for digital marketers. AI algorithms are able to generate customized marketing campaigns and advertisements based on the tastes and requirements of specific consumers by evaluating customer data. This degree of customization boosts client loyalty and conversion rates while also improving the consumer experience.

7.1.5 Marketing Campaign Automation and

Optimization

Financial companies can save time and money by implementing AI to automate and optimize several components of marketing campaigns. AI-powered solutions have the ability to plan and distribute advertisements on many platforms automatically, track the effectiveness of campaigns, and make real-time adjustments to maximize outcomes. Because AI handles the tedious and repetitive chores, marketers are free to concentrate on the creative and strategic components of their campaigns.

7.1.6 Taking Advantage of Social Media Marketing's Power

Social media platforms have developed into effective marketing tools that give financial institutions a more personal way to interact with their target audience. Financial institutions may customize their marketing messages and interact with clients more meaningfully by using AI to analyze social media data, spot patterns, and track customer sentiment. In addition to encouraging brand endorsement and loyalty, social media marketing can assist in creating a community around AI-driven financial services and products.

7.1.7 Creating Alliances with Financial Organizations

One way to promote AI-driven financial goods and services that benefit both parties is to work together with other financial institutions.

Financial startups can expand their customer base and brand recognition by collaborating with well-established institutions. Partnerships can also give access to important knowledge, resources, and routes of distribution, which can hasten the development and uptake of AI-driven financial solutions.

7.1.8 Public Speaking and Thought Leadership Engagements

Financial institutions can greatly increase their exposure and credibility by establishing thought leadership in the area of artificial intelligence in finance. Financial institutions can establish themselves as authorities on the subject by disseminating knowledge, research findings, and success stories via industry conferences, webinars, and public speaking engagements. Potential clients, financiers, and partners may be drawn to the organization as a result of its thought leadership, further enhancing its reputation and competitive edge.

7.1.9 Assessing and Quantifying Marketing Outcomes

In order to maximize return on investment and optimize future efforts, marketing strategies must be measured. Real-time data on important performance metrics, like click-through rates, conversion rates, and customer engagement, can be obtained through analytics systems driven by artificial intelligence. Financial institutions can improve their performance by identifying areas for improvement, making data-driven decisions, and fine-tuning their marketing strategy.

7.1.10: Using Content Marketing to Create a Community

Using content marketing to create a community around AI-powered financial services and solutions works well. Financial institutions can position themselves as reliable information sources by producing informative and valuable material, such as blog entries, articles, and videos. Through a variety of platforms, such as social media, email newsletters, and trade journals, this content can be disseminated, drawing in and retaining a devoted following.

To sum up, digital marketing and internet advertising are essential for promoting AI-driven financial services and goods. Financial institutions can target certain groups, tailor marketing messaging, increase their online presence, and enhance their marketing efforts by utilizing AI approaches. Financial firms can become industry leaders and create a community around their AI-driven products by forming alliances, leading thought leadership, and using content marketing. In the always-changing digital landscape, measuring and assessing marketing effectiveness is critical to attaining better outcomes and ongoing improvement.

7.2   Collaborations   with   Financial Establishments

Collaborations between financial institutions are essential for promoting innovation and acceptance in the quickly changing field of artificial intelligence in finance. There are several advantages to working with well-established companies in the field, such as having access to important resources, knowledge, and a larger clientele. This section examines the value of relationships with financial institutions and offers advice on how to start and maintain these alliances.

7.2.1 The Importance of Collaborations

AI-driven finance initiatives can greatly benefit from partnerships with financial institutions. The following are some of the main advantages of forming partnerships:

Data Access: Financial institutions have a wealth of important data, such as transaction histories, client profiles, and market statistics. Working together with these organizations can give you access to top-notch data sets, which can help you build AI models that are more reliable and accurate.

Financial institutions possess extensive domain knowledge and skill in a range of financial sectors, including regulatory compliance, investment strategies, and risk management. AI developers can make use of this knowledge and obtain important insights into the unique requirements and challenges of the finance industry by working with these institutions.

Validation and Credibility: AI-driven solutions gain legitimacy when partnered with reputable financial institutions. Gaining the trust of investors and consumers through the endorsement of a respectable organization can increase adoption and success rates.

Distribution Channels: Customer networks and distribution channels are well-established in financial organizations. By collaborating with them, you can gain access to a wider clientele, hastening the uptake and implementation of AI-powered financial services and products.

7.2.2 Forming Alliances
Careful strategy and execution are necessary for forming fruitful partnerships with financial institutions. Take into consideration these crucial

steps:

Find possible partners: Look for and find financial organizations that share your goals and objectives for AI-driven finance. Seek out organizations that are open to embracing new technology and have a history of innovation.

Articulate a Value Proposition: Make sure prospective partners understand the value that your AI product offers. Emphasize how your technology can help the organization with certain problems or issues it is facing, including increasing customer satisfaction, cutting expenses, or increasing efficiency.

Develop Relationships: Get in touch with the important financial institution decision-makers. Attend trade shows and social gatherings and hold conversations to establish rapport and trust. To gain credibility, show off your proficiency and understanding of finance and artificial intelligence.

Collaborative Approach: See partnerships as a team endeavor as opposed to a one-sided deal. Ask the financial institution for feedback and include them in the creation and improvement of your AI solution. This cooperative strategy raises the possibility of long-term success and cultivates a sense of ownership.

Legal and Regulatory Considerations: Before forming any collaborations with financial institutions, make sure that all legal and regulatory criteria are satisfied. To draft suitable contracts and agreements that safeguard the interests of all parties concerned, consult legal professionals.

7.2.3 Strengthening Alliances

For long-term success, it is crucial to foster and preserve partnerships with financial institutions once they have been formed. Here are some tactics to think about:

Frequent Communication: Keep lines of communication open and consistent with your partners. Give updates on your AI solution's development, exchange views, and solicit criticism. This constant communication improves collaboration and fosters trust.

Collaborative Innovation: Keep working together with your partners to investigate fresh prospects and creative applications of AI in the financial sector. To promote success and growth on both sides, encourage the exchange of ideas and knowledge.

Co-branding and co-marketing: Work together on marketing campaigns with financial institutions to showcase your AI-powered financial products. Collaborative webinars, thought leadership content, and co-branding initiatives can all help draw in more clients and raise awareness.

Training and assistance: To guarantee a seamless

integration and uptake of your AI solution, offer training and assistance to the financial institution's staff. This can involve continuing technical assistance, workshops, and training sessions.

Performance Evaluation: In cooperation with the financial institution, assess your AI solution's effectiveness on a regular basis. Gather input, track important performance metrics, and make the required changes to your solution to increase its efficacy.

7.2.4 Case Studies: Fruitful Collaborations
Let's examine two case studies to highlight the advantages and potential of collaborations with financial institutions:

Case Study 1: Risk Management Solution Powered by AI: A multinational bank joins with a fintech firm that specializes in AI-driven risk management solutions. The bank provides the company with access to its vast customer database and industry knowledge, which helps them create a very precise risk assessment model. Better risk management skills assist the bank by lowering losses and boosting regulatory compliance.

Case Study 2: Customer service solution powered by AI A top insurance carrier and an AI technology supplier collaborate to create an AI-powered customer support system. The system uses machine learning techniques and natural language processing to automate customer support requests and offer tailored advice. The insurance firm benefits from lower response times, more efficient operations, and happier customers as a result of the cooperation.

These case studies demonstrate how partnerships may revolutionize the financial sector by fostering innovation and yielding real advantages.

In conclusion, utilizing AI in finance to its fullest potential requires collaboration with financial institutions. AI-driven finance projects have the potential to accelerate their growth and adoption by utilizing the distribution channels, resources, and expertise of these institutions. Planning ahead, working together, and maintaining constant contact are necessary for forming and maintaining these partnerships. Effective collaborations can result in increased market reach, credibility, domain knowledge, and data access, all of which help propel the AI-driven financial revolution ahead.

7.3 Oral Publications and Thought Leadership
In the subject of artificial intelligence in finance, public speaking engagements and thought leadership are essential for building credibility and impact. It is crucial for you to actively participate in the industry as an author and subject matter expert and to take advantage of public speaking opportunities to promote your expertise. The significance of public speaking engagements will be discussed in this part, along with practical tips for using them to develop thought leadership in the AI-driven financial revolution.

7.3.1 Developing Contemplative Leadership
Establishing yourself as an authority and reliable source of information in the area of artificial intelligence in finance is the goal of thought leadership. You can get recognized in the industry and establish yourself as a thought leader by giving public speeches about your knowledge and

observations. The following tactics will assist you in developing thought leadership:

7.3.1.1 Find Appropriate Speaking Engagements
Look for and locate business events, conferences, and seminars that highlight artificial intelligence in banking. Seek out chances to present your knowledge and add to the conversations around this new area of study. To increase your network and reach, take into account both national and international events.

7.3.1.2 Create engaging topics for presentations.
Provide timely, pertinent presentation topics that tackle the main obstacles and possibilities in AI-driven finance. Make sure your presentations are tailored to your target audience's interests and needs in order to deliver insightful information and practical solutions. Here are a few ideas for presentation topics:

"The Future of AI in Financial Markets: Trends and Predictions"
"Unlocking the Power of AI in Investment Strategies"
"Personalized Financial Planning in the Age of AI"
"Navigating Complex Financial Data with AI: Techniques and Best Practices"
7.3.1.3 Distribute Practical Illustrations and Case Studies
Provide case studies and real-world examples to back up your presentations, showing how AI is being used in the banking industry.

Emphasize achievements and demonstrate how AI-driven tactics have improved results and changed financial organizations. This will support your credibility and offer concrete proof of AI's influence on the sector.

7.3.1.4 Work together with industry leaders.
Work together with other authorities and influential people in the financial AI space. Collaborative presentations, panel discussions, and co-writing articles and research papers are ways to accomplish this. Connecting with other reputable experts might help you build your network and improve your credibility.

7.3.2 Making the Most of Speaking Engagements in Public
Upon obtaining speaking engagements, it's critical to optimize the influence of your speeches. The following tactics will assist you in getting the most out of your public speaking appearances:

7.3.2.1 Create captivating and educational presentations.
Take the time to prepare interesting and well-organized presentations. Employ visual aids like graphs, charts, and infographics to highlight important ideas and help the audience understand difficult ideas. Use narrative strategies to draw in the audience and leave them with lasting impressions from your presentations.

7.3.2.2 Make your presentations specific to the

viewers.

Recognize the interests and demographics of your audience and adjust your presentations appropriately. To make your information relevant and easily readable, take into account the degree of technical proficiency and knowledge regarding artificial intelligence in finance. To promote involvement and a closer bond, include interactive features like Q&A sessions or live demos.

7.3.2.3 Make Use of Online and Social Media Channels

Make the most of social media and online platforms to increase the audience for your public speaking engagements. Post brief excerpts from your talks, important lessons learned, and ideas on social media sites like YouTube, Twitter, and LinkedIn. Encourage audience members to contribute their ideas and experiences by answering their queries and comments.

7.3.2.4 Connect and Establish Partnerships

Make the most of the networking opportunities that come with giving public speeches. Make connections with attendees, professionals in the field, and other speakers to grow your network. After meeting someone, get in touch with them to discuss future speaking engagements or joint ventures.

7.3.3 Assessing Outcome and Influence

It is crucial to set quantifiable objectives and monitor pertinent indicators in order to evaluate the effectiveness and impact of your speeches in public. Take a look at these metrics:

The number of speaking engagements that were obtained
Size and demographics of the audience
Degrees of participation during presentations (e.g., queries raised, conversations started)
Social media interaction and reach (likes, shares, comments, etc.)
Possibilities for partnerships or collaboration that result from giving speeches
You may evaluate the success of your public speaking endeavors and make necessary modifications to optimize your influence by monitoring these data.

To sum up, thought leadership and public speaking engagements are effective means of building reputation and influence in the AI finance space. Through speaking engagements, you may actively participate in the industry, establish yourself as an authority, disseminate your knowledge, and support the financial revolution powered by artificial intelligence. Don't forget to create interesting presentations, adjust your content for the audience, use internet and social media channels, and network with people in the field. By doing this, you may get the most out of your speeches in public and leave a lasting effect on the banking industry's use of AI.

7.4 Community Development and Social Media Marketing

Social media has become an essential component of our lives in the current digital era. It has completely changed the way we connect, communicate, and exchange information. Social media has given businesses—including those in the financial sector—new options for community development and marketing. In this section, we will discuss the value of social media marketing and how to use it to create a vibrant community centered around AI-driven finance.

7.4.1 Social Media Marketing's Power

There are billions of active users on social networking sites like Instagram, LinkedIn, Facebook, and Twitter. These platforms offer businesses the chance to interact in real time with a large audience. Social media may be a very effective strategy for building a brand, generating leads, and raising awareness when it comes to AI marketing in the banking industry.

The capacity of social media marketing to target particular interests and demographics is one of its main benefits. Businesses can guarantee that the proper audience receives their message by utilizing advanced targeting options. If you are marketing a robo-advisor service, for instance, you can focus on people who have expressed interest in investing or personal finance subjects.

The affordability of social media marketing is an additional advantage. Social media networks are a more cost-effective approach to promoting your AI-driven finance book than traditional advertising channels. With a set budget, you may launch focused ad campaigns, monitor the effectiveness of your ads, and make real-time adjustments to maximize your outcomes.

7.4.2 Formulating a Plan for Social Media

A clear plan is essential for utilizing social media for AI marketing in the finance industry. Take into consideration these crucial steps:

Determine Who Your Target Market Is

Establishing who your target audience is is essential before you start using social media marketing. Which individuals are most likely to find your book interesting? Are they investors, finance professionals, or just people who want to learn more about finance? Knowing your target market will enable you to create content and messaging that appeal to them.

Select the appropriate channels.
Social media networks are not created equally. Every platform has a distinct user base and set of features. Selecting the platforms that work best for your target market and marketing objectives is crucial. For instance, Instagram can be a better option to reach a younger audience, but LinkedIn would be a better fit if you are targeting finance experts.

Make interesting content.
You must provide interesting material if you want to draw in readers on social media. Videos, infographics, essays, and even interactive tests may fall into this category. It's important to add value to your audience and position yourself as an authority on AI-driven finance. To keep your audience interested, don't forget to combine user-generated content, promotional pieces, and instructional information.

Interact with the People in Your Audience
Social media is about more than just spreading your message; it's also about establishing a rapport with your followers. Answer queries, reply to remarks, and take part in pertinent conversations. Engaging with your audience can help you establish credibility and trust, both of which will be important in creating a successful book community.

Make use of partnerships and influencers.
On social media, influencer marketing has grown in popularity. Find prominent figures in the finance sector who have the same values as your book and have a sizable fan base. Work together to spread the word about your work and attract more readers. To increase your reach and credibility, think about partnering with financial institutions or other pertinent groups.

7.4.3 Civic Engagement

Long-term success requires cultivating a community around your AI-driven finance book. A vibrant community may offer insightful criticism, encourage word-of-mouth recommendations, and act as brand ambassadors. The following are some methods for creating a community:

Make a customized hashtag.
User-generated material can be promoted, and a sense of community can be fostered using a branded hashtag. Urge your readers to utilize the hashtag when discussing their opinions, queries, or personal experiences pertaining to your work. This will encourage a sense of community among your audience in addition to assisting you in monitoring and interacting with user-generated content.

Organize live Q&A events.
Set up live Q&A sessions on social media sites so that users may ask queries and receive prompt responses. You can connect with your audience

directly in this interactive style, answering their questions and offering insightful commentary. Because attendees can engage with one another during the session, it also contributes to the development of a sense of community.

Promote content created by users.
One of the best ways to create a community around your book is through user-generated content. Invite your readers to contribute their thoughts, opinions, or even original works of art that are connected to your book. Your audience will feel more invested as a result, and engagement will also rise.

Provide discounts or exclusive content.
Offer discounts or access to special content as a way to thank your community members. This could take the form of extra chapters, webinar access, or a price break on upcoming publications or occasions. You may cultivate brand supporters and brand loyalty by adding value to your community.

In summary
A strong marketing plan for AI in finance must include social media marketing and community development. Businesses may reach a larger audience, interact with their target market, and create a vibrant community around their AI-driven finance book by utilizing the power of social media channels. It is imperative to have a clearly defined social media strategy, provide

captivating content, and participate actively with your audience in order to cultivate a sense of community and promote sustained success.

REAL-WORLD EXAMPLES OF AI IN FINANCE

8.1 Case Study 1: AI-Powered Trading Strategies

In this case study, we will examine how AI can be used to create trading techniques that have the potential to completely transform the financial industry. Trade techniques driven by AI have the potential to improve trade efficiency, streamline decision-making, and increase investor returns. We will explore the many methods and approaches that went into creating these tactics and look at actual instances of their effective application.

8.1.1 Overview of Trading Strategies Powered by AI

Artificial intelligence (AI)-powered trading strategies use cutting-edge algorithms and machine learning techniques to examine enormous volumes of financial data, spot trends, and make wise trading decisions. These tactics seek to minimize human bias, automate the trading process, and take advantage of real-time market possibilities. Artificial intelligence (AI) systems can quickly and accurately produce trading signals and execute trades by combining historical data, market indicators, and predictive analytics.

8.1.2 Using Machine Learning Methods in Trading Plans

Creating trading methods driven by AI requires a strong understanding of machine learning. These methods allow for the detection of patterns and trends that can be utilized to forecast future moves in the market by training algorithms on past data. Several machine learning approaches that are frequently employed in trading strategies include:

8.1.2.1 Guided Education

Supervised learning algorithms are designed to produce predictions or classifications based on labeled historical data. These algorithms can be trained to forecast stock prices, spot market trends, or categorize market circumstances in trading. Supervised learning algorithms utilize past price movements and associated indicators to provide trading signals that adhere to predetermined rules.

8.1.2.2 Learning via Reinforcement

Through experimentation and interaction with their surroundings, reinforcement learning algorithms pick up new skills. These algorithms can be trained to maximize profits and minimize risks in order to optimize trading strategies. Reinforcement learning algorithms are capable of learning to make the best trading decisions in a variety of market scenarios through the simulation and evaluation of trades.

8.1.2.3 In-Depth Learning

Neural networks and other deep learning algorithms are able to recognize intricate patterns and correlations in data. Deep learning algorithms have the potential to assess vast amounts of financial data in trading, such as sentiment on social media, news articles, and price fluctuations. Deep learning algorithms are able to produce trade signals and highly accurate forecasts by identifying significant traits from many data sources.

8.1.3 Practical Illustrations of AI-Powered Trading Techniques

Let's look at some actual instances of AI-driven trading tactics that have performed well in the financial markets:

8.1.3.1 Trading at High Frequency (HFT)

A trading technique known as "high-frequency trading" depends on the utilization of strong computers and algorithms to carry out numerous trades in a matter of milliseconds. Artificial intelligence (AI)-driven HFT tactics use machine learning techniques to instantly assess market data and make trading decisions. These tactics seek to capitalize on tiny pricing differences and inefficiencies in the market.

8.1.3.2 Trading Quantitatively

Statistical analysis and mathematical models are used by quantitative trading strategies to find trading opportunities. Artificial intelligence (AI)-driven quantitative trading strategies employ machine learning algorithms to examine past data, spot trends, and produce trade signals. Trading a variety of financial items, such as stocks, bonds, commodities, and currencies, is possible with these tactics.

8.1.3.3 Emotional Dissection

Sentiment analysis is a method for assessing the sentiment of the market by examining news stories, social media posts, and other textual data. Algorithms for sentiment analysis driven by AI are capable of processing vast amounts of text data and extracting information pertaining to sentiment. These algorithms are able to produce trading signals based on the general sentiment of the market by examining the sentiment of market participants.

8.1.4 Advantages and Difficulties of Trading Strategies Powered by AI

Financial institutions and investors can profit from AI-powered trading techniques in a number of ways.

Enhanced trading efficiency: AI systems are able to assess enormous volumes of data and quickly and accurately execute deals, which enhances trading efficiency.

Improved decision-making: Artificial intelligence (AI) systems have the capacity to analyze large amounts of data and spot trends that human traders might miss, which results in better trading choices.

Decreased human bias: Trading tactics driven by AI have the potential to lessen human emotion and bias in trading, resulting in more unbiased and logical decision-making.

But there are drawbacks to using AI-powered trading tactics as well:

Data availability and quality: In order for AI algorithms to produce precise predictions, they need timely and high-quality data. In the financial markets, ensuring data availability and quality can be difficult.

AI algorithms are susceptible to overfitting, a phenomenon in which they exhibit good performance on historical data but are unable to adapt to novel market situations. In trading methods driven by AI, controlling model risk is essential.

Ethics and regulatory considerations: A number of ethical and regulatory issues, including accountability, transparency, and fairness, are brought up by the use of AI in trading.

8.1.5 In summary

AI-powered trading techniques can improve trade efficiency, accelerate decision-making, and increase investor returns—all of which have the potential to completely transform the financial industry. These strategies make use of sophisticated algorithms and machine learning techniques to evaluate large volumes of financial data, spot trends, and make well-informed trading decisions. To guarantee the ethical and responsible application of AI in trading, it is crucial to solve the issues around model risk, data quality, and regulatory concerns.

8.2 Case Study 2: AI-Powered Apps for Personal Finance

In this case study, we will examine how artificial intelligence (AI) is used in the creation of personal finance apps. These apps use artificial intelligence (AI) technology to provide consumers with investment recommendations, budgeting help, and personalized financial advice. Through the use of sophisticated algorithms and data analysis, these applications seek to enable users to reach their financial objectives and manage their money more skillfully.

8.2.1 Overview of AI-Powered Personal Finance Applications

Since people are looking for quick and easy solutions to manage their money, personal finance applications have grown in popularity. Numerous functions are available with these apps, such as goal-setting for finances, budgeting tools, investment management, and cost tracking. These apps' AI integration enables them to deliver consumers personalized recommendations and insights based on their own financial objectives and circumstances.

8.2.2 AI Methodologies in Apps for Personal Finance

AI methods are essential to the operation of apps for personal finance. Let's examine some of the main AI methods employed in these applications.

Machine learning: To find patterns and trends in user data, machine learning algorithms evaluate and interpret the data. These algorithms can offer tailored advice for budgeting, saving, and investing by examining spending patterns, revenue streams, and financial objectives.

Natural Language Processing (NLP): NLP allows user input in natural language to be understood and interpreted by personal financial apps. With the ability to interact with the app via text or voice commands, users can input financial data more easily and intuitively and obtain pertinent insights.

Predictive analytics: To forecast future patterns and outcomes, predictive analytics algorithms examine previous financial data. By anticipating possible dangers and possibilities, these algorithms can assist users in making well-informed decisions on debt management, savings, and investments.

Robo-Advisory: Robo-advisory is an automated

investment management technique that builds and maintains investment portfolios using artificial intelligence (AI) algorithms. These algorithms provide individualized investment recommendations and maximize portfolio performance by taking into account variables including risk tolerance, investment objectives, and market conditions.

8.2.3 Advantages of Personal Finance Apps Powered by AI

Users gain from the incorporation of AI in personal financial apps in a number of ways, including:

Personalized Financial Advice: AI-powered personal finance apps are able to offer customized financial guidance according to a user's financial circumstances, risk tolerance, and personal objectives. Users' financial well-being can be enhanced and decisions made more intelligently with the aid of this tailored advice.

Effective Budgeting and Expense Management: Artificial intelligence algorithms have the ability to examine spending trends and classify costs autonomously, facilitating users in monitoring their expenditures and pinpointing areas where they may economize. Additionally, to assist users in sticking to their spending limits, these apps can offer real-time notifications and alerts.

Investment advice: Personal finance apps can

offer consumers investment advice based on their risk tolerance and financial goals by utilizing AI approaches. These suggestions, which might aid consumers in optimizing their investment plans, are supported by data-driven analysis.

Financial Goal Defining and Monitoring: Users can get help from AI-powered personal finance apps in defining and monitoring their financial objectives. These applications can offer insights on how to accomplish particular goals, like saving for a down payment on a home or making retirement plans, by examining income, spending, and savings patterns.

8.2.4 Difficulties and Things to Remember
Although AI-driven personal finance apps have many advantages, there are drawbacks and things to keep in mind as well.

Sensitive financial data is collected and stored by personal finance applications, which raises privacy and security concerns. Strong security measures must be in place for these apps in order to shield user data from breaches or unwanted access.

Accuracy and Reliability: The AI algorithms utilized in personal finance apps must be accurate and reliable. Users depend on these apps to help them make financial decisions, so any mistakes or inaccuracies could have serious repercussions. Algorithms must be tested and observed frequently to guarantee their efficacy.

Ethical Data Use: User data must be handled by personal financial apps in an open and moral manner. Users should be aware of how their data is being used, and app developers should follow privacy laws and policies.

8.2.5 Practical Illustrations
In recent years, a number of AI-powered personal finance apps have grown in popularity. Here are a few instances:

Mint: Mint is a popular personal finance app that assists users in managing their money by using artificial intelligence approaches. It provides tools for budgeting, investment tracking, and cost tracking, among other things. Mint uses user data analysis to offer individualized financial health suggestions and insights.

Acorns: Acorns is an investing program that rounds up user purchases and invests any leftover change using AI algorithms. Personalized investment portfolios based on user preferences and financial objectives are also provided by the app.

Betterment: Betterment is a robo-advisory platform that builds and maintains financial portfolios using artificial intelligence algorithms. In order to offer individualized investment suggestions, it takes into account variables including risk tolerance, time horizon, and financial objectives.

Conclusion

AI-powered personal financial apps have the power to completely change how people handle their money. These apps are able to offer effective budgeting tools, investment recommendations, and individualized financial advice by utilizing AI techniques including machine learning, natural language processing, and predictive analytics. But in order to guarantee the credibility and dependability of these applications, it is imperative that issues pertaining to data privacy, accuracy, and ethical issues are addressed. AI-driven personal finance apps will probably become more and more important in helping people reach their financial objectives as technology develops.

8.3 AI in Risk Management: Case Study No. 3

In this case study, we will examine the use of AI in risk management in the financial industry. Any financial institution's operations must include risk management since it entails locating, evaluating, and reducing possible risks that can have an effect on the company's reputation and financial stability. Financial organizations now have access to strong tools and strategies that can improve their risk management procedures, thanks to developments in AI technology.

8.3.1 Recognizing and Evaluating Hazards
Accurately identifying and promptly assessing hazards is one of the main issues in risk management. Conventional risk management techniques frequently rely on laborious manual procedures and human judgment, which can be error-prone and time-consuming. However, artificial intelligence (AI) can automate and streamline these procedures, making it possible for financial institutions to discover and evaluate risks more quickly.

Financial statements, market data, news stories, social media feeds, and enormous volumes of data from other sources can all be analyzed with the help of artificial intelligence (AI) techniques like machine learning and natural language processing. Artificial intelligence systems are able to discern patterns, trends, and abnormalities in this data that could point to possible hazards. Machine learning algorithms, for instance, are capable of analyzing financial data from the past to find trends that point to fraud or market manipulation.

8.3.2 Risk Management Using Predictive Analytics

Another area where AI may greatly improve risk management in the financial sector is predictive analytics. Artificial intelligence (AI) algorithms can forecast future hazards and their possible effects on the company by utilizing sophisticated statistical models and historical data. This makes it possible for financial institutions to proactively reduce these risks before they manifest.

For instance, AI systems are capable of forecasting the probability of a financial crisis or a market decline by examining macroeconomic data and past market data. Financial institutions can preserve their assets and reduce possible losses by implementing risk mitigation methods, adjusting their investment portfolios, and allocating resources more wisely in light of these projections.

8.3.3 Fraud Identification and Avoidance

Financial institutions are exposed to a large amount of fraud risk, and artificial intelligence (AI) can be extremely helpful in identifying and stopping fraud. Large amounts of transactional data may be instantly analyzed by AI algorithms, which search for trends and abnormalities that might point to fraud. AI systems are able to recognize unusual activity and send out notifications for additional research by tracking transactions over time and comparing them to past data.

Furthermore, with the use of sophisticated

authentication and verification methods, AI can aid in the prevention of fraud. For instance, the identity of people carrying out financial transactions can be confirmed using biometric authentication techniques like fingerprints or facial recognition. To verify the legitimacy of the transaction, AI systems can evaluate biometric data and compare it to profiles that have been stored.

8.3.4 Scenario analysis and stress testing

Because they enable financial institutions to evaluate their resistance to unfavorable market circumstances and future shocks, stress testing and scenario analysis are crucial instruments in risk management. By modeling different situations and examining their possible effects on the organization's financial health, AI can improve these procedures.

Financial organizations can create realistic scenarios based on past data and current market situations by utilizing machine learning algorithms. The organization's susceptibility to various risks, such as market volatility, loan defaults, or liquidity shortages, can then be evaluated using these scenarios. Financial organizations are able to make well-informed judgments and create effective risk mitigation plans because of AI algorithms' ability to assess simulated data and offer insights into prospective impacts on important financial KPIs.

8.3.5 Risk reporting and regulatory compliance

In the financial industry, adhering to regulations is a crucial part of risk management. Financial institutions must comply with a number of rules and requirements, many of which are intricate and time-consuming. These procedures can be made more efficient and compliant with AI, which also lessens the demand on human resources.

To ascertain an organization's compliance status, artificial intelligence (AI) algorithms can examine regulatory documents and extract pertinent information. Financial institutions can make sure they are compliant with the most recent regulatory standards and modifications by automating this process. By producing accurate and thorough reports based on the organization's risk exposure and mitigation methods, AI may also help with risk reporting.

8.3.6 AI's advantages and difficulties in risk management

A number of advantages come with using AI in risk management, including increased efficiency and accuracy, better risk detection and assessment, proactive risk reduction, and simplified regulatory compliance. To guarantee that AI is successfully included in risk management, there are, nevertheless, certain obstacles that must be overcome.

A primary obstacle is the accessibility and caliber of the data. Large amounts of high-quality data are necessary for AI algorithms to produce precise forecasts and insights. In order for financial institutions to effectively train and validate AI models, they must make sure that they have access to pertinent and trustworthy data sources.

The interpretability and explainability of AI algorithms are another difficulty. It can be difficult to comprehend how these algorithms make decisions as AI grows more powerful and complex. Financial organizations may find it challenging to defend and explain their risk management plans to stakeholders and regulators due to this lack of openness.

Furthermore, while using AI in risk management, ethical issues must also be taken into account. Financial institutions must make sure AI algorithms are impartial, transparent, and fair—that is, they shouldn't discriminate against any one person or group. To prevent illegal access to or exploitation of sensitive financial information, data privacy and security issues must also be addressed.

Notwithstanding these difficulties, artificial intelligence (AI) offers greater advantages in risk management than disadvantages. Financial organizations that use AI technology can obtain a competitive edge by strengthening their overall financial stability and streamlining their risk management procedures.

In summary, AI has the power to completely transform risk management in the financial industry. Financial institutions may improve their risk identification, assessment, and mitigation procedures by utilizing AI techniques like machine learning, natural language processing, and predictive analytics. In addition, regulatory compliance, risk reporting, stress testing, and scenario analysis can all benefit from AI. Even though there are obstacles to overcome, AI's advantages for risk management make it a useful tool for financial institutions in the complicated and quickly changing financial world of today.

8.4 Case Study 4: Using AI to Identify Fraud

Fraud in the financial sector is a chronic and expensive issue. Conventional techniques for detecting fraud frequently fail to quickly detect and stop fraudulent activity. But as artificial intelligence (AI) has progressed, new avenues for addressing this obstacle have opened up. Artificial intelligence (AI)-driven fraud detection systems have proven to be incredibly successful in identifying and stopping fraudulent activity, saving financial institutions billions of dollars annually.

8.4.1 AI for Fraud Detection Overview

In the financial industry, fraud can take many different forms, such as insider trading, credit card fraud, money laundering, and identity theft. These actions damage people's and organizations' finances, in addition to undermining confidence in the financial system. Artificial intelligence (AI)-driven fraud detection systems use sophisticated analytics and machine learning algorithms to find trends and abnormalities in vast amounts of data, allowing for the early discovery and stop of fraudulent activity.

8.4.2 Using Machine Learning to Identify Fraud

Systems for detecting fraud powered by artificial intelligence heavily rely on machine-learning algorithms. By analyzing past data, these algorithms are able to spot trends and abnormalities that can point to fraud. Labeled datasets, which distinguish between fraudulent and non-fraudulent transactions, can be used to train supervised learning systems. Conversely, anomalies in data can be found using unsupervised learning algorithms without the requirement for labeled instances.

8.4.3 Feature engineering and data preprocessing

Effective fraud detection systems must first do data pretreatment and feature engineering before implementing machine learning techniques. To guarantee the quality and consistency of raw data, data preparation includes cleaning and altering it. Choosing and developing pertinent elements that can aid in differentiating between fraudulent and non-fraudulent transactions is known as feature engineering. Transaction quantities, timestamps, geographic locations, and patterns of consumer behavior are a few examples of these features.

8.4.4 Methods for Identifying Fraud
AI-driven fraud detection systems use a range of methods to spot and stop fraudulent activity. Among the methods that are frequently employed are:

8.4.4.1 Finding anomalies
Algorithms for anomaly detection are used to spot transactions or actions that greatly depart from the usual. From historical data, these algorithms identify the typical patterns and highlight any transactions that have peculiar characteristics. The detection of new or emerging fraud trends can be greatly aided by anomaly detection.

8.4.4.2 Analysis of Networks
Techniques for network analysis examine the links and interconnections that exist between different financial system elements. These methods can find suspicious trends and unearth connections between dishonest people by looking at the network of exchanges and interactions.

8.4.4.3 Analysis of Behavior

The goal of behavior analysis approaches is to recognize patterns of deviation from an entity's or person's regular behavior. These methods identify anomalous activity that can point to fraudulent activity by examining past data and consumer behavior.

8.4.4.4 Interpreting Natural Language (NLP)

Text-based interactions and other unstructured data can be analyzed using natural language processing (NLP) techniques to spot fraudulent activity. NLP algorithms are capable of identifying conversations that seem suspicious or efforts to deceive or manipulate people by examining the sentiment and content of communications.

8.4.5 Practical Applications of AI in Fraud Detection

Numerous financial institutions and businesses have successfully used AI-powered fraud detection systems. PayPal is one well-known example, which uses AI algorithms to instantly examine millions of transactions and identify fraudulent activity. Through the application of machine learning and behavioral analytics, PayPal has successfully decreased fraud rates and safeguarded the financial assets of its users.

Another illustration is Citibank, which tracks credit card transactions using AI-based fraud detection tools. Citibank is able to swiftly detect and stop suspicious transactions, saving money for both the bank and its clients, by examining transaction patterns, consumer behavior, and historical data.

8.4.6 AI's advantages and difficulties in detecting fraud

The use of AI in fraud detection has various advantages for businesses and financial institutions. Among them are:

Increased accuracy: AI-driven fraud detection systems have the capacity to accurately evaluate vast amounts of data, which lowers the number of false positives and false negatives.

Real-time detection: Because AI algorithms are able to examine transactions in real-time, fraudulent activities can be identified and stopped as soon as they happen.

Scalability: AI systems are very scalable and successful in identifying new fraud trends since they can manage massive volumes of data and adjust to shifting fraud patterns.

Nevertheless, applying AI to fraud detection is not without its difficulties. Among them are:

Data security and privacy are issues since AI systems must have access to private financial information.

Interpretability: It might be tough to comprehend the logic underlying AI systems' fraud detection judgments since they can be intricate and complicated to grasp.

Adversarial attacks: Data manipulation and vulnerability-based fraudsters may try to trick AI systems, necessitating ongoing monitoring and model adaptation for fraud detection.

8.4.7 Upcoming Developments in AI Fraud Detection

Technology breakthroughs and the growing expertise of fraudsters are driving constant evolution in the field of artificial intelligence for fraud detection. Future developments in this area could include:

Deep learning: Because deep learning methods, such as neural networks, can automatically identify intricate patterns and relationships in data, they are being investigated for use in fraud detection.

The goal of explainable AI is to increase system trust and transparency by creating AI models that offer justifications for their fraud detection judgments.

Collaborative intelligence: To identify and stop cross-institutional fraud, AI systems can gain from cooperation and information exchanged between financial institutions and other organizations.

To sum up, AI-driven fraud detection tools have the potential to completely transform the battle against financial fraud. These technologies have the ability to identify and stop fraudulent activity in real time, saving financial institutions billions of dollars by utilizing machine learning algorithms and advanced analytics. To assure the ethical and successful application of AI in fraud detection, however, issues including interpretability, adversarial assaults, and data privacy and security need to be addressed. The application of AI to fraud detection has enormous potential to improve safety and security in the financial ecosystem, as long as technology keeps developing.

ACTIONABLE STRATEGIES FOR AI-DRIVEN FINANCE

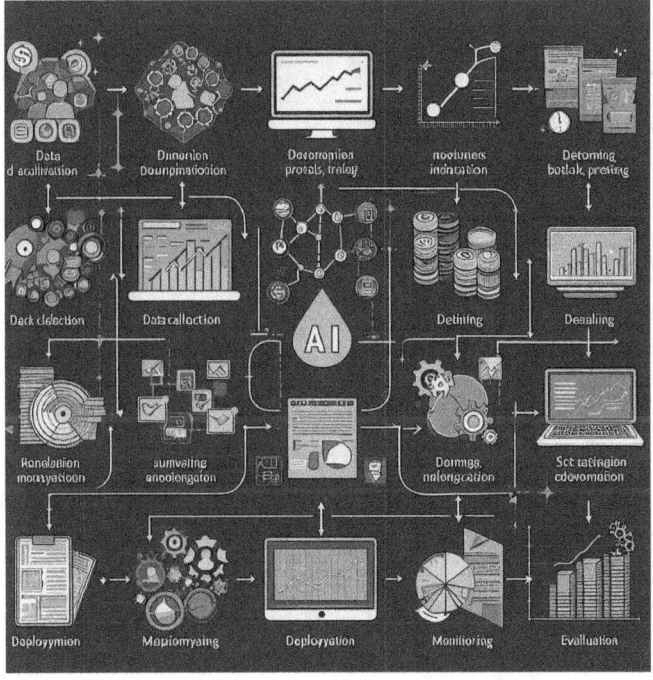

9.1 Financial Institutions' Use of AI

The financial sector could undergo a transformation thanks to artificial intelligence (AI), which can improve decision-making procedures, increase productivity, and make it possible to create cutting-edge financial goods and services. A thorough grasp of the technology and its ramifications, as well as meticulous planning and strategic considerations, are necessary for the use of AI in financial institutions. The main actions and factors to be taken into account when successfully integrating AI into financial institutions will be discussed in this section.

9.1.1 Evaluating Organizational Readiness
Financial institutions must determine if they are prepared to accept and use AI technology before starting the process of implementing it. This evaluation includes a look at the company's data management capabilities, technological infrastructure, and workforce availability. Before deploying AI, it is imperative to have a thorough grasp of the organization's current situation and to identify any gaps that need to be filled.

9.1.2 Clearly Outlining Use Cases and Objectives
Financial organizations need to specify precise goals and use cases where AI can be useful in order to guarantee a successful AI implementation. This entails carrying out a comprehensive examination of the problems, difficulties, and prospects

facing the firm. Financial institutions should concentrate their efforts on areas where artificial intelligence (AI) can have the biggest impact, such as risk management, fraud detection, customer service, or investment strategies, by identifying specific use cases.

9.1.3 Gathering and Preparing Data

The fuel that keeps AI systems running is data. For AI models to be able to access high-quality data, financial institutions must have a strong strategy in place for gathering and preparing data. Finding pertinent data sources, cleaning and preparing the data, and guaranteeing data security and privacy are all necessary for this. In order to improve existing datasets and obtain new insights, financial institutions can also think about utilizing external data sources, such as social media feeds or market data.

9.1.4 Constructing the Infrastructure for AI

A strong and scalable infrastructure is needed to support the creation, application, and upkeep of AI models when implementing AI in financial institutions. This infrastructure consists of software tools and frameworks for data processing, model training, and inference, in addition to hardware resources like servers and GPUs. Financial institutions have two options: they can use cloud-based services that offer AI capabilities on demand, or they can develop their own AI infrastructure.

9.1.5 Building AI Frameworks
Choosing the right algorithms and methods that fit the specified goals and use cases is a crucial step in the development of AI models. Financial institutions have access to a multitude of artificial intelligence (AI) techniques, such as computer vision, natural language processing, machine learning, and deep learning. Model training and validation, feature engineering, and optimization are all steps in the development process. For AI models to be accurate and effective, it is imperative that their performance be regularly assessed.

9.1.6 Coordination and Implementation
Financial organizations must incorporate the AI models into their current systems and procedures after they are built. In order to guarantee smooth integration and compatibility with legacy systems, extensive collaboration with IT teams is required. In order to manage growing data quantities and user interactions, financial institutions also need to take the scalability and dependability of the AI models into account. To find and fix any problems or performance degradation, testing and monitoring must be done on a regular basis.

9.1.7 Control and Observance
A strong governance framework is necessary for the ethical and responsible application of AI in financial organizations. Financial institutions should set forth explicit rules and regulations

pertaining to security, privacy, and the openness of data. It is crucial to adhere to legal standards, such as those pertaining to knowing your customer (KYC) and anti-money laundering (AML). To detect and reduce any possible dangers connected to the application of AI, audits and risk assessments should be carried out on a regular basis.

9.1.8 Ongoing Education and Development

Since the field of artificial intelligence is continuously changing, financial institutions must adopt a culture of ongoing learning and development. This entails keeping abreast of the most recent developments in AI technology, keeping an eye on market trends, and making investments to expand AI expertise within the company. To remain at the forefront of AI innovation, financial institutions should also encourage cooperation and knowledge exchange with outside partners, such as academic institutions or research centers.

9.1.9 Employee Training and Change Management

Using AI in financial institutions necessitates a major cultural shift as well as change management initiatives. It is crucial to explain to staff members the advantages of AI and include them in the implementation process. Comprehensive training programs should be offered by financial institutions to ensure that staff members have the skills needed to operate with AI technologies. Training in data analytics, AI algorithms, and moral issues in AI-driven decision-making are all included in this.

9.1.10 Calculating ROI and Success

Financial institutions must create key performance indicators (KPIs) and set up a framework for calculating return on investment (ROI) in order to assess the success of AI adoption. Metrics like cost savings, efficiency benefits, customer satisfaction, or risk reduction are examples of KPIs. Frequent tracking and evaluation of these indicators will help inform future decision-making and offer insights into how well AI is being implemented.

The process of implementing AI in financial organizations is intricate and multidimensional. It necessitates a calculated strategy, meticulous preparation, and a thorough comprehension of the goals and competencies of the company. Financial institutions can leverage artificial intelligence (AI) to propel innovation, improve decision-making, and provide superior financial services to their clientele by heeding the guidelines provided in this section and taking into account the pertinent factors.

9.2 Developing Financial Products Powered by AI

Artificial intelligence (AI) has become a potent instrument in the quickly changing financial sector, capable of revolutionizing conventional financial goods and services. Financial solutions powered by AI have the ability to completely transform the market by offering individualized suggestions, automated processes that are more efficient, and projections that are more accurate. We will look at the main ideas and methods for creating AI-powered financial solutions in this part.

9.2.1 Recognizing the Needs of the Market

Prior to starting the process of developing financial products powered by AI, it is essential to comprehend market demands and pinpoint pain areas that AI may help with. Gaining meaningful insights into the unique possibilities and problems faced by the financial sector can be achieved through comprehensive market research and active engagement with potential users and customers.

You can determine the areas where AI may bring the greatest benefit by comprehending the needs of the market. For instance, AI-powered robo-advisors have become more well-known for offering automated investing guidance based on the risk tolerance and goals of specific individuals. In a similar vein, AI-powered credit scoring models have completely transformed the lending sector by making loan approval procedures more precise and effective.

9.2.2 Data Gathering and Preparation Access to pertinent and high-quality data is necessary for the development of AI-driven financial products. Preparing and gathering data are essential stages in the development process. Data collection from a variety of sources, such as external data providers, financial markets, and customer transactions, is crucial.

After being gathered, the data must be cleansed, preprocessed, and formatted so that AI algorithms can use it. This calls for activities like feature engineering, normalization, and data cleaning. The performance and dependability of the AI models will be greatly impacted by the quality and accuracy of the data.

9.2.3 Selecting Appropriate AI Methods
The choice of suitable AI approaches that meet the

unique criteria and aims is critical to the success of AI-driven financial solutions. Machine learning, deep learning, natural language processing, and reinforcement learning are just a few of the AI techniques that are available.

Regression, classification, and clustering are examples of machine learning algorithms that can be used for tasks like fraud detection, risk assessment, and predictive modeling. Image and speech recognition are two examples of tasks that deep learning, a subset of machine learning, excels at, involving complex patterns and unstructured data.

Techniques for natural language processing (NLP) make it possible to glean insightful information from textual material like financial reports, social media messages, and news stories. Automated document summarizing, sentiment analysis, and sentiment tracking in news can all be done with NLP.

Conversely, sequential decision-making applications like algorithmic trading and portfolio optimization are well suited for reinforcement learning.

9.2.4 Model Construction and Assessment

The creation and training of AI models come after the selection of AI methodologies. This includes deciding on the right algorithms, fine-tuning the model's parameters, and assessing the model's effectiveness.

Making sure the models are trained on a representative and diverse dataset is essential during the model development phase. By doing this, biases and overfitting are reduced, which helps prevent erroneous predictions and untrustworthy outcomes.

Iteratively testing the model's performance on a different dataset and making necessary adjustments to the model based on the assessment's findings constitute the process of model evaluation. Setting up strong assessment criteria that correspond with the particular objectives of the financial product is crucial.

9.2.5 Implementation and Coordination
The next stage is to include the AI models in the financial product and implement them in a real-world setting after they have been created and assessed. This entails integrating the AI models with already-in-use technologies, like customer-facing apps, trading platforms, and investment management tools.

Ensuring the scalability, dependability, and security of the AI models is essential at the integration and deployment stages. This covers factors including data privacy, high availability, and real-time data processing.

9.2.6 Ongoing Evaluation and Enhancement
The process of creating financial solutions

powered by AI is ongoing and calls for constant observation and development. It is crucial to track how well the AI models function in actual situations and get input from clients and users.

Through consistent performance monitoring, you may detect any problems or constraints with the AI models and implement the appropriate fixes. This could entail updating the model parameters, retraining the models with new data, or implementing fresh AI methods as they become available.

9.2.7 Ethics and Regulation Concerns

Regulation and ethics must be carefully considered while developing AI-driven financial products. To guarantee the legitimacy and dependability of the financial product, compliance with legal standards is crucial, including data privacy laws and financial regulations.

Fairness, accountability, and transparency are a few ethical issues that must be taken into account. AI models ought to be created without prejudice or discrimination, and they ought to give concise justifications for their choices.

9.2.8 Cooperation and Joint Ventures

Developing AI-powered financial products frequently calls for cooperation and joint ventures with a range of stakeholders. This can entail collaborating with financial institutions, technology suppliers, or data providers. Working together can open up access to important information, knowledge, and resources that will hasten the creation and uptake of financial products powered by artificial intelligence.

You may access pre-existing networks and distribution channels, build credibility, and connect with a larger audience by utilizing partnerships. Regulatory and compliance issues can also be addressed through collaborations by utilizing the knowledge and experience of well-established financial institutions.

To sum up, making AI-powered financial products requires a deep understanding of what the market wants, good data preparation and collection, smart choice of AI technique, strong model development and evaluation, easy integration and deployment, ongoing monitoring and improvement, and following all ethical and legal rules. By implementing these tactics, financial institutions can leverage AI's potential to develop cutting-edge and revolutionary financial solutions that satisfy changing consumer demands and advance the sector.

9.3 Ethical Issues in the Use of AI

It is critical to address the ethical issues raised by the application of artificial intelligence (AI) as its use in the finance sector grows. Although artificial intelligence (AI) has many advantages, it also has drawbacks that should be carefully considered. In this part, we will go over some of the most important ethical issues that practitioners and financial institutions need to be aware of when implementing AI technology.

9.3.1 Explainability and Transparency

The lack of explainability and transparency in AI algorithms is one of the main ethical issues regarding their use in the financial sector. A lot of artificial intelligence models, including deep learning neural networks, are referred to as "black boxes" since their judgments are based on intricate correlations and patterns that are challenging to understand. Concerns over accountability and the capacity to comprehend and justify the logic underlying AI-driven judgments are raised by this lack of transparency.

Financial institutions should work to create AI models that are accessible and comprehensible in order to address this problem. This can be accomplished by applying interpretable AI strategies, including decision trees or rule-based systems, which offer concise justifications for the choices made by the AI algorithms. To maintain openness and facilitate auditing, more efforts should be taken to record and monitor the information, characteristics, and algorithms used in AI models.

9.3.2 Bias and Fairness

The possibility of bias in AI algorithms is a crucial ethical factor to take into account before adopting AI. AI algorithms might be biased and exhibit discriminating behaviors because they are trained on previous data. AI systems have the potential to reinforce and magnify current discrimination and inequality in financial decision-making processes if these biases are not addressed.

Financial institutions should make sure that the training data they utilize is representative and diverse in order to reduce bias in AI systems. To eliminate any potential biases, the data must be properly chosen and preprocessed. It is also important to regularly audit and monitor AI systems in order to spot any biases that might develop over time and take appropriate action.

9.3.3 Data security and privacy

Adoption of AI in finance frequently entails gathering and analyzing enormous volumes of sensitive and personal data. Data security and privacy are brought up by this. It is imperative for financial institutions to establish comprehensive policies and procedures for data protection in order to preserve the privacy and confidentiality of client information.

Before collecting and using someone's data for AI purposes, it is imperative to get their informed consent. Techniques for encryption and data anonymization should also be used to safeguard sensitive data. Financial institutions must also put in place suitable security measures to thwart illegal access and data breaches, as well as adhere to applicable data protection laws, such as the General Data Protection Regulation (GDPR).

9.3.4 Responsibility and Accountability

The use of AI in finance creates concerns around liability and responsibility for judgments made by AI systems. In conventional financial decision-making, decisions might be held accountable to specific people or organizations. As AI systems start making judgments on their own, though, it gets harder to assign blame.

Financial institutions should specify the roles and duties of those involved in the development and implementation of AI systems in order to address this problem and create clear lines of accountability. AI systems must be monitored and audited in order to make sure they are operating as planned and to spot any potential problems or biases.

9.3.5 Human Guidance and Management

Even though AI may streamline and automate a lot of financial procedures, human monitoring and control must still be maintained. Financial organizations need to make sure AI solutions are made to support human judgment rather than completely replace it. When necessary, human specialists should be able to evaluate and override judgments made by AI.

Financial institutions should also spend money on staff education and training to make sure that workers are equipped with the know-how to comprehend and utilize AI technologies. As a result, they will be able to work with AI systems more successfully and use the insights that AI algorithms provide to make wise decisions.

9.3.6 Ongoing Assessment and Observation

The deployment of AI raises ongoing ethical issues that need to be continuously observed and assessed. Financial organizations should set up procedures and guidelines for routinely evaluating the moral implications of their AI systems. This entails keeping an eye out for biases, assessing the effect on stakeholders, and dealing with any new ethical issues that may arise.

To guarantee adherence to moral principles and legal requirements, AI systems should undergo routine audits and evaluations. To promote accountability and openness in the deployment of AI, financial institutions should also actively interact with regulators, industry experts, and the general public.

In conclusion, there are a lot of advantages and prospects associated with the use of AI in finance, but there are also significant ethical issues to be aware of. For AI to be used responsibly and ethically, financial institutions and practitioners need to place a high priority on openness, equity, privacy, responsibility, human oversight, and ongoing monitoring. The financial sector can leverage AI's potential while upholding business ethics and fostering trust by tackling these issues.

9.4 Prospects and Trends for AI Finance in the Future

Although artificial intelligence (AI) has already

had a big influence on the financial sector, its full potential has yet to be reached. New trends and opportunities are emerging as technology keeps developing, further revolutionizing the way the banking industry functions. We will look at a few potential future developments and trends in AI finance in this part.

9.4.1 Improved Client Relationship

Improving the customer experience is one of the main areas where artificial intelligence will keep progressing. In the banking industry, AI-powered chatbots and virtual assistants are already widely used to provide clients with prompt, individualized answers to their questions. But there are even more interesting things to come in the future.

Artificial intelligence (AI) systems will get better at comprehending and responding to complicated client needs as machine learning and natural language processing continue to progress. These technologies will be able to suggest customized goods and services, offer individualized financial advice, and even predict the future demands of the user. This degree of individualized care will increase client retention and pleasure while also fostering loyalty.

9.4.2 Sophisticated Risk Control

AI has the potential to significantly improve risk assessment and mitigation, which is a crucial component of the banking industry. Conventional risk models might not adequately represent the complexity and dynamic nature of today's financial markets because they are based on past data and predetermined rules.

Artificial intelligence (AI) has the ability to evaluate enormous volumes of data in real-time, spot trends and abnormalities, and forecast possible hazards with high accuracy. By adapting and learning from fresh data, machine learning algorithms help financial institutions keep ahead of developing dangers and make better judgments. This proactive approach to risk management will increase overall financial stability and reduce losses.

9.4.3 Comprehending Artificial Intelligence

Transparency and explainability are becoming increasingly important as AI gets more widely used in the finance sector. Deep learning neural networks are among the many AI models that are sometimes regarded as "black boxes," making it difficult to comprehend how they make judgments. Adoption may be seriously hampered by this lack of interpretability, particularly in highly regulated fields like finance.

The creation of AI models that can clearly explain their decisions—known as explainable AI models—will be the main focus of future developments in AI finance. Financial institutions will be able to guarantee responsibility, win over customers, and comply with regulations thanks to this. Additionally, explainable AI will support justice and moral decision-making by assisting in the detection of possible prejudices and discriminatory behaviors.

9.4.4 Financial Quantum Computing

A new technology called quantum computing has the power to completely transform a number of sectors, including finance. Financial firms can tackle difficult optimization problems and more precisely simulate financial scenarios because of the extraordinary speed at which complicated calculations can be performed by quantum computers.

More advanced risk analysis, pricing models, and portfolio optimization techniques will be possible in the future, thanks to quantum computing. It will also make it possible to design encryption methods that are resistant to quantum e-rays, which will increase the security of financial transactions. Even though quantum computing is still in its infancy, it has enormous potential for the financial sector and will probably influence how AI is used in the field going forward.

9.4.5 Regulatory Compliance and Ethical AI

Ethical issues and regulatory compliance will become more crucial as AI becomes more commonplace in the financial industry. Financial institutions will have to make sure AI technologies are developed and used in an equitable, open, and responsible manner. This entails dealing with problems including prejudice, discrimination, and privacy issues.

The creation of frameworks and rules for moral AI and regulatory compliance will be the main focus of future developments in AI finance. This will entail putting in place strong governance procedures, auditing and evaluating AI systems, and setting industry standards. Financial firms can gain the trust of the public, regulators, and customers by putting ethical AI first.

9.4.6 Cooperation between AI and Humans

Even if AI has the ability to automate a lot of financial processes, human-AI collaboration will be a hallmark of the future. AI will complement human abilities, allowing finance professionals to concentrate on higher-value tasks and make more informed judgments.

To make sure that their staff members have the skills needed to collaborate with AI systems, financial institutions will need to make investments in upskilling them. This entails gaining a thorough grasp of data analysis, critical thinking, and AI technologies. AI and human cooperation will improve the effectiveness and efficiency of financial processes, which will eventually benefit financial institutions and their clients.

9.4.7 AI in Finance Becomes More Democratic

A wider spectrum of financial firms are finding

it easier to acquire AI technology as it develops. We may anticipate the democratization of AI in finance in the future, as startups and smaller businesses use AI to compete with more established, bigger corporations.

The adoption and implementation of AI solutions by financial institutions of all sizes will be facilitated by advancements in cloud computing, open-source software, and AI platforms. In addition to leveling the playing field, this will open up fresh possibilities for disruption and innovation in the finance sector.

9.4.8 Strengthened Cybersecurity
Cybersecurity will become even more important as AI and digital technologies become more and more prevalent in the financial sector. Financial institutions will have to make investments in cutting-edge cybersecurity systems driven by AI in order to guard against ever-changing risks like fraud, data breaches, and cyberattacks.

Artificial intelligence (AI) can improve threat intelligence, spot suspicious behavior patterns, and assist in the real-time detection and response to security events. Financial institutions may fortify their defenses and protect sensitive client data by utilizing AI in cybersecurity.

In summary, there are a ton of fascinating opportunities for AI in banking in the future. Some of the trends and opportunities that will influence the future of AI finance are increased consumer experiences, advanced risk management, explainable AI, quantum computing, ethical AI, human-AI collaboration, democratization of AI, and improved cybersecurity. Financial institutions will be well-positioned to prosper in the AI-driven financial revolution if they adopt these trends and make use of AI technologies.

CONCLUSION AND KEY TAKEAWAYS

10.1 An Overview of AI Methods in Finance

In this chapter, we will give a thorough overview of the AI methods that are transforming the finance sector. These methods have the power to completely change the way financial institutions run by giving them the ability to make better judgments, work more efficiently, and provide better customer service. Readers will have the skills necessary to successfully navigate the AI-driven financial revolution by comprehending these AI strategies.

10.1.1 Artificial Intelligence

Within artificial intelligence, machine learning is the field dedicated to creating models and algorithms that allow computers to learn and make decisions without explicit programming. Machine learning techniques find wide-ranging applications in finance, such as fraud detection, risk assessment, market trend analysis, and portfolio optimization. Machine learning algorithms are capable of identifying trends and producing very accurate forecasts by evaluating enormous amounts of financial data.

10.1.2 Understanding Natural Language (NLP)

A subfield of artificial intelligence called natural language processing, or NLP, is concerned with how computers and human language interact. NLP techniques are applied in finance to analyze and interpret unstructured data from sources like financial reports, social media messages, and news articles. Through the extraction of pertinent data from these sources, natural language processing (NLP) algorithms can yield insightful information for sentiment research, market analysis, and risk assessment.

10.1.3 In-depth Analysis

A branch of machine learning known as "deep learning" is devoted to creating artificial neural networks with architecture and functionality modeled after the structure and operations of the human brain. Deep learning algorithms can extract complicated information and produce precise predictions because they can automatically learn hierarchical representations of data. Deep learning methods are applied in finance to tasks including credit scoring, fraud detection, and picture identification.

10.1.4 Learning via Reinforcement

A subfield of machine learning called reinforcement learning is concerned with teaching agents how to behave in a way that maximizes rewards. Techniques for reinforcement learning can be applied to finance to create trading methods that adjust to shifting market conditions. Reinforcement learning algorithms have the ability to maximize trading decisions and enhance overall performance by utilizing lessons learned from previous experiences and providing feedback in the form of rewards or penalties.

10.1.5 Automation of Robotic Processes (RPA)

Thanks to a technology called robotic process automation (RPA), software robots can now automate repetitive and rule-based tasks. RPA can be utilized in the banking industry to automate tasks including data input, reconciliation, and report creation. RPA helps financial companies increase productivity, lower errors, and devote resources to higher-value operations by relieving human resources of repetitive duties.

10.1.6 Algorithms for Genetics

Natural selection serves as the inspiration for genetic algorithms, which are methods of optimization. Genetic algorithms can be used in finance to determine the asset combination that maximizes returns while minimizing risk, hence optimizing investment portfolios. Genetic algorithms can search a vast search area and converge on the best answers by mimicking the evolution process.

10.1.7 Networks of Bayesian

Directed acyclic graphs are used in Bayesian networks, which are probabilistic graphical models to depict the relationships between variables. Bayesian networks can be applied to finance to perform tasks like risk assessment, fraud detection, and credit scoring. Bayesian networks are capable of producing precise forecasts and offering insightful information by simulating the relationships between variables and taking previous knowledge into account.

10.1.8 Collaborative Education

The process of combining several models to generate predictions or judgments is known as ensemble learning. Ensemble learning techniques can be applied to finance to increase prediction robustness and accuracy. Ensemble learning methods can lessen the impact of individual model faults and produce more dependable results by combining the predictions of several models.

10.1.9 Analysis of Time Series

A statistical method called time series analysis is used to examine and predict data points gathered over an extended period of time. Time series analysis techniques are used in finance for forecasting interest rates, stock prices, and other financial variables. Time series analysis algorithms are able to forecast future time points with high accuracy by spotting patterns and trends in the historical data.

10.1.10 Analysis of Networks

The technique of network analysis is centered on examining the connections among the entities inside a network. Techniques for network analysis can be applied in finance to find transaction trends, spot fraud, and evaluate systemic risk. Risk management and regulatory compliance can greatly benefit from the insights that network analysis algorithms can offer by examining the dynamics and structure of financial networks.

To sum up, the AI methods covered in this chapter have the power to completely transform the financial sector. Financial institutions may make better decisions, automate procedures, and offer more individualized services with the help of these technologies, which range from deep learning and reinforcement learning to machine learning and natural language processing. Readers may remain ahead of the AI-driven financial transformation and seize new chances for success by comprehending and utilizing these AI strategies.

10.2 Crucial Takeaways and Reader Strategies

We will highlight the most important learnings and tactics from the AI revolution in finance in this book's concluding section. We have discussed several AI approaches and their uses in the financial industry in the earlier chapters. Let's now summarize the key lessons learned and offer readers doable plans they can use to improve their personal financial situation.

10.2.1 Lean Into AI's Potential in Finance

The first important realization is the enormous potential AI has to completely transform the banking sector. Artificial intelligence (AI) methods like sentiment analysis, pattern recognition, and predictive analytics can offer insightful market data and assist in making wise investment decisions. Financial organizations and individual investors can improve their financial results and obtain a competitive advantage by utilizing AI.

10.2.2 Recognize the Advantages and Difficulties

It's critical to comprehend the advantages and difficulties of artificial intelligence in the financial sector. Artificial intelligence (AI) has the potential to increase productivity, accuracy, and profitability, but it also has hazards and ethical issues. Readers can safely navigate the AI landscape and minimize any potential drawbacks by being aware of these factors.

10.2.3 Incorporate AI into investment plans

Using AI to develop investing strategies is one of the most significant uses of technology in finance. Robo-advisors and algorithmic trading systems are examples of automated investment platforms that can improve portfolio allocation, quickly execute trades, and efficiently manage risk. If readers want to improve their investing performance and reach their financial objectives, they should think about implementing AI-driven investment techniques.

10.2.4 Use AI to Customize Financial Planning

AI has a big place in customized financial planning as well. People may efficiently prepare for retirement, analyze costs, set realistic financial objectives, and make smart budgets by utilizing AI-based tools and algorithms. In order to improve their money management and make wise judgments, readers should investigate AI-driven financial planning tools.

10.2.5 Leverage Data's Power

The fuel that keeps AI systems running is data. Readers should concentrate on gathering, preparing, and evaluating pertinent financial data in order to fully utilize AI in finance. Methods like data mining, natural language processing, and data visualization can reveal hidden patterns and offer insightful information. Readers can obtain a competitive edge and make better decisions by utilizing the power of data.

10.2.6 Talk About Ethical Issues

It is critical to address ethical concerns as artificial intelligence (AI) becomes increasingly common in banking. When it comes to adopting AI, transparency, justice, and accountability should come first. It is imperative for readers to ascertain that the design and implementation of AI systems conform to ethical norms and regulatory mandates. Financial organizations and individuals may uphold the integrity of the financial system and foster trust by placing a high priority on ethics.

10.2.7 Adopt a Wholesome Marketing Approach

A complete marketing plan is essential for anyone trying to promote financial goods or services driven by artificial intelligence. Public speaking engagements, social media marketing, joint ventures with financial institutions, and online advertising can all be used to efficiently reach the target demographic and raise awareness. To establish thought leadership and create a community around their AI-driven financial solutions, readers can think about implementing these marketing methods.

10.2.8 Take Notes from Actual Cases

Examples from the real world offer important insights into the useful uses of AI in finance. Readers can learn from the experiences of others and find inspiration by reading case studies and success stories. Numerous case studies that demonstrate the effective application of AI in trading methods, risk management, fraud detection, and personal finance apps are included in the book. The readers ought to examine these instances and derive significant insights to implement in their individual financial pursuits.

10.2.9 Keep up with Emerging Trends

Staying ahead of future trends is critical in the ever-evolving field of artificial intelligence in finance. Readers ought to stay informed on the most recent developments in the industry, laws, and AI technology. Readers may recognize fresh opportunities and modify their approaches in response to the evolving AI market in finance by becoming informed.

In conclusion, both financial institutions and private investors stand to gain greatly from the AI revolution in finance. Readers can position themselves at the forefront of the AI-driven financial revolution by embracing AI, comprehending its advantages and disadvantages, putting AI-driven strategies into practice, personalizing financial planning, utilizing data, addressing ethical issues, implementing a thorough marketing strategy, keeping up with emerging trends, and learning from real-world examples. The essential knowledge and techniques in this book will enable readers to successfully traverse the intricate world of artificial intelligence in finance and reach their financial objectives.

10.3 Concluding Remarks about the AI-Powered Financial Revolution

There is no denying that AI is driving a financial revolution that is having a significant influence on the industry. As we come to the end of this book, it's critical to ponder the most important lessons learned and the long-term effects of this revolutionary technology.

10.3.1 Accepting Adaptability and Change

AI adoption in finance necessitates a mentality shift and an openness to change. Financial institutions need to be aware of how AI might completely transform their business processes and be willing to try out novel approaches and cutting-edge tools. To remain ahead of the curve in this ever-changing environment, it is imperative to cultivate a culture of flexibility and ongoing learning.

10.3.2 Humans and Machines Working Together

Even if AI has the ability to automate a lot of financial chores and procedures, it's crucial to remember that people are still essential. The best applications of AI in finance will combine human and machine intelligence, utilizing each other's advantages. AI systems must be guided by human skill, intuition, and ethical judgment to ensure responsible decision-making.

10.3.3 The Adoption of AI with Ethical Considerations

Ethical issues are becoming more crucial as AI is used in banking more and more. Transparency, equity, and accountability must be given top priority in financial institutions' AI systems. It's critical to eliminate biases, protect data security and privacy, and lay forth precise rules for the appropriate application of AI. Regulations and ethical frameworks should be created to control the use of AI in the financial industry.

10.3.4 Ongoing Assessment and Observation

AI systems in finance should be regularly assessed and monitored to make sure they are working well and to reduce any hazards. To find and fix any biases, mistakes, or vulnerabilities in AI algorithms, routine audits and evaluations are required. Continuous training and reassessment of AI models is necessary to adapt to shifting consumer demands and market conditions.

10.3.5 The Significance of Governance and Data Quality

The availability of high-quality data is crucial for the application of AI in banking. For financial organizations to guarantee the quality, correctness, and dependability of their data, they need to invest in strong data collection, preprocessing, and governance procedures. Since AI algorithms can only be as good as the data they are trained on, data quality needs to be a primary concern.

10.3.6 Opportunities and Difficulties with Regulation

There are regulatory obstacles associated with the use of AI in finance. Regulators must create frameworks that balance innovation and consumer protection while keeping up with technological changes. Working together, regulators, financial institutions, and AI experts can create norms and guidelines that encourage the financial sector to deploy AI responsibly.

10.3.7 AI's Role in Finance in the Future

The use of AI in finance has a bright future. We may anticipate even more automation, efficiency, and precision in financial procedures as AI technologies develop. Chatbots and virtual assistants driven by AI will advance in sophistication and be able to offer each user individualized financial recommendations and assistance. Artificial intelligence (AI) will be used increasingly frequently in risk management and fraud detection, improving the stability and security of the financial system.

10.3.8 Education and Skill Development's Role

Education and skill development are essential if AI is to be fully utilized in the banking industry. The information and abilities required for financial professionals to comprehend and effectively use AI technologies must be acquired. Upskilling and constant learning will be necessary to remain competitive in the AI-driven financial sector and to adjust to the industry's shifting expectations.

10.3.9 Accepting the Financial Revolution Driven by AI

In conclusion, there are a plethora of

opportunities for financial institutions, experts, and individuals in the AI-driven financial revolution. Financial institutions can automate investing methods, obtain insightful market data, and offer individualized financial planning services by utilizing AI approaches. Adopting AI should be done cautiously, taking ethical issues into account, making sure the data is accurate, and encouraging human-machine cooperation. The AI-driven financial revolution has the potential to empower people and improve the financial industry if the proper policies, tactics, and mentality are put in place.

APPENDIX

11.1 Communal AI Terminology

The field of artificial intelligence (AI) is one that is constantly developing and includes many different methods and ideas. It is crucial that you become familiar with the jargon used in this field as you explore the realm of AI in finance. An overview of some of the most important AI terms and concepts that you will come across in this book is given in this part.

11.1.1 Artificial Intelligence

A branch of artificial intelligence called machine learning (ML) focuses on creating models and algorithms that let computers learn and make decisions without explicit programming. ML algorithms gain experience over time and become more proficient by learning from data. ML algorithms come in various forms, such as reinforcement learning, unsupervised learning, and supervised learning.

11.1.2 In-depth Education

The structure and operation of the human brain serve as inspiration for the ML subfield of deep learning. Artificial neural networks (ANNs) with several layers of interconnected nodes, or neurons, are used in this process. Deep learning systems can extract complicated patterns and features by automatically learning hierarchical representations of the input. Deep learning has shown impressive results in a number of fields, such as speech and image recognition.

11.1.3 Intricate Networks

Computational models, known as neural networks, are based on the architecture and operation of biological brain networks. They are made up of layers of networked nodes, or neurons. Every neuron takes in input signals, processes them, and then outputs a signal. Because neural networks can recognize intricate patterns and relationships in data, they are an excellent choice for applications like financial forecasting, natural language processing, picture and audio recognition, and more.

11.1.4 Processing Natural Language

A subfield of artificial intelligence called natural language processing, or NLP, is concerned with how computers and human language interact. Computers can now comprehend, interpret, and produce meaningful and practical human language thanks to NLP approaches. NLP is utilized in many different applications, including voice assistants, chatbots, sentiment analysis, and language translation. NLP can be applied to the analysis of financial news, reports, and social media data in the finance domain in order to obtain knowledge and make defensible decisions.

11.1.5 Learning via Reinforcement

One kind of machine learning (ML) is called reinforcement learning (RL), in which an agent learns how to interact with its surroundings in order to maximize a reward signal. Through trial and error, the agent gains knowledge and receives feedback in the form of incentives or sanctions, depending on its performance. Applications of reinforcement learning (RL) include autonomous driving, robots, and game playing. RL is useful in finance for creating risk assessment models, portfolio management systems, and trading techniques.

11.1.6 Trading Algorithms

The term "algorithmic trading" describes the automation of the purchase and sale of financial products, including derivatives, stocks, and bonds, through the use of computer algorithms. Because algorithmic trading systems can execute trades quickly and often, they can profit from short-term price fluctuations and market inefficiencies. In order to create prediction models, recognize trading signals, and enhance trading methods, algorithmic traders frequently employ AI techniques like machine learning and reinforcement learning.

11.1.7 Cyber-Mentor

Digital platforms known as "robo-advisors" offer automated portfolio management and investment guidance. These platforms evaluate risk profiles, analyze financial data, and suggest appropriate investment plans to individual investors using AI techniques like ML and NLP. Because of their low fees, accessibility, and capacity to offer individualized financial advice based on each client's goals and preferences, robo-advisors have become more and more popular in recent years.

11.1.8 Analytics for Predictive

Statistical models and machine learning

algorithms are used in predictive analytics to examine previous data and forecast future occurrences or results. Predictive analytics is a useful tool in finance that may be used to quantify credit risk, forecast market trends, and spot fraudulent activity. Predictive analytics can offer insightful information and assist financial organizations in making defensible judgments by utilizing AI approaches.

11.1.9 Information Extraction

Finding patterns, connections, and insights within big databases is known as data mining. To extract meaningful information from unprocessed data, statistical methods, machine learning algorithms, and visualization tools are used. Data mining is a useful tool in finance that may be used to spot anomalies, segment clients, find market trends, and improve investment methods. AI methods like machine learning and natural language processing are frequently applied in data mining to find hidden patterns and produce useful insights.

11.1.10 Large-scale Data

Large and complicated datasets that are difficult to manage, process, or analyze with conventional data processing methods are referred to as "big data." Big Data is defined by its truth, volume, velocity, and variety. Big Data in finance refers to a broad category of data sources, such as transactional data, news articles, social media data, and market data. AI methods for analyzing big data and deriving insightful knowledge for decision-making include machine learning (ML) and natural language processing (NLP).

11.1.11: Moral Points to Remember

An essential component of AI in finance is ethical consideration. The financial industry is seeing an increase in the use of AI technology, so it is imperative that ethical concerns about privacy, security, bias, accountability, and transparency be addressed. Fairness, nondiscrimination, consumer data protection, and upholding the integrity and confidence of financial institutions are all ethical issues in AI-driven finance. To control the application of AI in finance, financial organizations and legislators must create moral standards and regulatory frameworks.

Some of the typical AI terms you will see throughout this book are introduced in this section. Gaining an understanding of these concepts will provide you with a strong basis on which to explore the different AI approaches and tactics covered in the upcoming chapters. You will learn more about how artificial intelligence (AI) is changing the finance sector as you read on, as well as how you may use these technologies to your advantage in the coming financial revolution.

11.2 Phrases and Ideas in Finance

To successfully navigate the intricacies of the finance business, one must be familiar with a wide range of terminology and concepts. A dictionary of financial terms and concepts often used in the field of AI-driven finance is provided in this appendix.

11.2.1 Resource

Any resource or piece of property with economic worth that can be held or controlled by a person, business, or government entity is referred to as an asset. Intangible assets like stocks, bonds, and intellectual property can also be considered assets, as can tangible ones like real estate, cars, and equipment.

11.2.2 Accountability

A responsibility is a duty or debt owed to a third party by a person or an organization. It is a claim against the debtor's assets and may be made in relation to credit card debt, mortgages, loans, or other types of debt.

11.2.3 Fairness

Equity is the ownership stake in a business or piece of real estate. It is determined by deducting liabilities from assets, and it may be expressed as retained earnings, preferred stock, or common stock. The remaining worth of the business or property after all debts and obligations have been settled is subject to equity holders' claims.

11.2.4 ROI, or return on investment

A financial metric called return on investment (ROI) is used to assess how profitable an investment is. It is computed as a percentage by dividing the net return from an investment by the investment's original cost. Investors use return on investment (ROI) as a significant metric to evaluate the effectiveness and profitability of their investments.

11.2.5 Hazard

Risk is the possibility of suffering a loss or not being confident that a desired result will be reached. In the world of finance, risk is a necessary component of investment and is usually connected to the erratic and unpredictable nature of financial markets. To reduce and manage the possible risks connected to their assets, investors and financial institutions employ a variety of risk management strategies.

11.2.6 Blending in

Spreading investments over several assets, industries, or geographical areas is known as diversification, and it is a risk management technique used to lessen the influence of any one investment on the portfolio as a whole. Investors may be able to lower their risk of loss and raise their chances of making money by diversifying their holdings.

11.2.7 Arrangement

An individual's or an organization's collection of investments is referred to as a portfolio. A wide range of assets, including real estate, mutual funds, equities, bonds, and other financial instruments, may be included. Managing a portfolio usually aims to achieve a certain investment objective, like minimizing risk or maximizing profits.

11.2.8 Steadiness

The degree of change or fluctuation in the price or value of a financial instrument or market is measured by its volatility. Higher volatility is indicative of a greater likelihood of price swings and uncertainty, and it is frequently employed as a risk indicator. When making financial selections, traders and investors must take volatility into account.

11.2.9 Availability

The ease with which a security or asset can be purchased or sold on the market without significantly altering its price is referred to as liquidity. Illiquid assets could take longer to sell or might need a discount to draw in buyers, whereas highly liquid assets can be quickly turned into cash. When evaluating the risk and possible return of an investment, liquidity is a crucial component to take into account.

11.2.10 Investment
Financial resources, or assets used to produce revenue or sustain economic activity, are referred to as capital. It can consist of money, assets, real estate, and other types of wealth. To finance operations, investments, and other financial activities, capital is a vital component of financial markets and is utilized by people, corporations, and governments alike.

11.2.11 Rate of Interest
The cost of borrowing money or the return on investment for lending money is expressed as an interest rate. It is usually charged or paid annually and is stated as a percentage. Interest rates have a significant impact on borrowing costs, investment returns, and the state of the economy as a whole in the financial markets.

11.2.12: The Inflation
The rate at which prices for goods and services are generally rising and, as a result, the currency's purchasing power is declining is known as inflation. Over time, inflation devalues money and can have a big impact on interest rates, investment returns, and the state of the economy. In order to make well-informed financial decisions, authorities and investors keep a close eye on inflation rates.

11.2.13 Statement of Financial Position
An official record of a person, business, or government's financial actions and status is called

a financial statement. An entity's assets, liabilities, and cash flows are all shown in detail by the income statement, balance sheet, and cash flow statement that are usually included. Creditors, investors, and other stakeholders use financial statements to evaluate the stability and health of an entity's finances.

11.2.14 Credit Rating A credit rating is a determination of a person, group, or government's creditworthiness. Credit rating agencies assign it based on their assessment of the entity's capacity to pay back its debts and commitments. Lenders, investors, and other financial institutions use credit ratings to assess the risk involved in making a loan or investing in a certain company.

11.2.15 The Law of Finance
The laws, rules, and regulations that control how financial markets and institutions operate are collectively referred to as financial regulations. It is intended to safeguard the interests of consumers and investors while advancing the financial system's fairness, stability, and openness. At both the national and international levels, regulatory bodies and agencies uphold financial regulations.

11.2.16 Adherence to the Standards
Compliance is the term used to describe how people, businesses, and financial institutions follow the law, rules, and industry standards. It entails putting policies, processes, and controls

in place to make sure that things are done in compliance with the relevant laws and regulations. Maintaining the integrity and reputation of financial institutions depends on compliance, which is a crucial component of financial operations.

11.2.17 Fintech

Fintech, an acronym for financial technology, describes the application of innovation and technology to the provision of financial services and goods. It covers a broad range of applications, including blockchain, artificial intelligence, robo-advisors, online payments, and mobile banking. Fintech has upended established financial institutions and has the power to completely change how money is exchanged.

11.2.18 The cryptocurrency

Cryptocurrency is a type of virtual or digital money that runs without the help of a central bank and uses cryptography for security. It is transparent, safe, decentralized, and built on blockchain technology. Some well-known cryptocurrencies are Ethereum, Ripple, and Bitcoin. Cryptocurrencies are gaining a lot of attention and might completely change the banking sector.

The essential financial terms and concepts that are pertinent in the context of AI-driven finance can be understood in part by using this glossary. To properly understand the complexities of the financial sector and utilize AI in finance, it is critical to keep investigating and learning about these ideas.